The
Numerology
of
Names

The Numerology of Names

Laureli Blyth

BLANDFORD

Acknowledgments

I would like to thank Tony for his inspiration and help, and Van and Anne for their guidance

Decorative motifs from *Persian Designs and Motifs for Artists and Craftsmen* by Ali Dowlatshahi, Dover Publications, Inc. (1979)

A BLANDFORD BOOK

First published in the UK 1996 by Blandford
A Cassell Imprint

CASSELL PLC
Wellington House
125 Strand
London WC2R 0BB

First published in Australia in 1995 by Kangaroo Press Pty Ltd

Distributed in the United States by Sterling Publishing Co., Inc.
387 Park Avenue South, New York, NY 10016-8810

British Library Cataloguing-in-Publication Data
A catalogue entry for this title is available from the British Library

ISBN 0-7137-2639-9

Printed in Australia by Australian Print Group

Contents

Dedicated with love to Heidi and Tom

Foreword

Names are more than mere labels. Your name is a very important key to understanding yourself as well as the first element of your identity. It sets the tone to how you conduct yourself and how you respond to the ever-changing world around you. Your name gives you authority, power and dominion, e.g. Heidi's car—Heidi's house—Heidi's job. It sets you apart from others, giving you your identity. It also influences how others react to you.

There are many books that can tell you the literal meaning of a name or its original meaning, often hundreds of years old, e.g. Andrew comes from a Greek word meaning manly, Miller refers to someone's long ago occupation, MacDonald means 'son of Donald'. These definitions have lost their original depth of meaning over the years and now people are interpreting names in more esoteric ways.

Numerology is the most accurate and effective form of character analysis from names. In the teachings of numerology a name is likened to a vehicle or tool that we have brought into this lifetime from the accumulated experiences of previous lifetimes. It gives us the means to successfully travel life's pathway in our own unique manner, using our special characteristics, talents and abilities. Often, however, we do not fully understand our talents until we awaken to our true identity. This mode of transportation through life involves not just the physical self but manifests itself also as a particular energy that vibrates at a distinctive rate.

You can see this vibration in different types of people; some are highly strung and some are laid back while others travel their path on an even keel. We all have strengths to bring out and weaknesses to overcome which are all a part of our energy vibration.

We learn at school that names are nouns; however, through numerology names come alive with individual meaning and become adjectives, full of description. Although we may share a name with another person (how many John Smiths are there in the world, for example?), the numerological total for our birthdate combined with our birth name reveals the 'pathway' which many of us can spend our lifetime searching for. This pathway, which I refer to as a 'birth blueprint', is uniquely created and tailor-made just for you. It is the map so many people wish they had and it *is* readily available, just awaiting the desire to find it and the awakening of the true identity.

No matter under what circumstances you were named, who named you, even if you neither like nor ever use that name, your name is the key to the mystery of you. Discovering your name's individual energies stimulates you to work with the principles of those energies and sets you on your pathway.

'Who am I?' 'What is my purpose in life?' 'Can I find direction and happiness?'

Do you wish to understand yourself and others around you? This book will answer these questions for you using numerology's simple method of name and birthdate correlation.

Our first conscious desire is to know and understand our self with complete honesty. Although few of us realise it, we all have a map of ourselves we were born with; it is found in our numerology chartings. Your search and ultimately your path to who you are can be revealed by knowing this truth and working with the principles of this ancient science. Numerology will reveal your energy vibrations and clarify your pathway.

Introduction

There are many books on numerology that illustrate the principles of this discipline; they use the numbers from 1 to 9 with some references to karmic numbers and a few master numbers (11, 22 and 33). Most of these books explain the birth path or birth date and its relevance to a person's thoughts and behaviour. Few devote anything to a person's name, which is as important as a birth date. None of them, I believe, extend the interpretations to the number 99, as I do in this book. The other area that receives little or no attention is the potential of double and triple numbers.

We are more than a 1 or a 2, or any other single number. Often people tell me they are a 3, for example, very proud of this information. But a true worker in this field would want to know all the facts, asking, 'In what area are you a 3, and what was the total number before it was reduced?' The detailed interpretation tells the true story of the person. Saying you are a 3 is like saying you are a Taurus when you have no knowledge of your rising sign or where your other planets are.

After many years of practice and study in numerology I came to the realisation that the information contained in names and double numbers was vital to a true character delineation. Once I became awakened to the intense potential of deeper meanings my perception and my work became enhanced. As happens to all of us when we are ready for more understanding, the answers came forth. In 1988 the book *Spiritual Light Vibrations* by Jeanne came to me. It validated my work and made we aware that we are able to continue working with the revelations that the numbers have to offer. What was known as the truth a hundred or even twenty years ago can now be expanded on for more awareness and enlightenment.

As we come to the doorway to the twenty-first century I notice the increasing number of new and different names coming into the world. Interpreting these names, numerologists will be ever more useful as pioneers in a new age of understanding and awareness to which humanity is rapidly awakening. We will all need to gain insight into who we are and what our purpose is in the rapidly-changing future.

This book may be the doorway which will open to help you on your journey to your spiritual discovery of Self.

1   What is Numerology?

Numerology is an extremely old and esoteric science that dates back to the ancient early civilisations. Pythagoras, who lived around 550 BC in Greece, was a student of numerology; in his school he taught the philosophy of numbers on which I base my studies and chart readings. As the teachings of numerology are brought further out into the open we draw on the information revealed in those ancient times to help us deal more easily with our modern everyday world. The more we learn the more is revealed.

The method used in this book to reach the true character analysis of a person is the Pythagorean formula, based on converting the individual elements of a name to numbers.

	1	2	3	4	5	6	7	8	9	11	22
Alpha-Numeric *Conversion* *Grid*	A	B	C	D	E	F	G	H	I	K	V
	J		L	M	N	O	P	Q	R		
	S	T	U		W	X	Y	Z			

Webster's *New Twentieth Century Unabridged Dictionary* defines numerology as: 'A system of occultism built around numbers, especially those giving birth dates, and those which are the sum of letters in one's name, etc.; divination by numbers.'

Numerology's object is the study and interpretation of the numbers in names and birth dates and how they relate to each person's individual energy vibrations. This gives us more complete self-knowledge, through which we can work to discover hidden talents, eradicate failings and reach a more fulfilling level of self expression and realisation of ideals. Numerology records and expresses your name's vibrations through numerical values.

A very popular form of divination, numerology is interpreted through an awareness of the rhythms and cycles of the universe. Every number has its own unique energy vibration which corresponds to a specific human character trait. Each letter has its equivalent in a number. A person can be a thinker or a doer, ambitious or lazy, motherly or a hermit—there are countless combinations depending on the sum of their name.

For instance, the name Adam adds to a numerology value of 10, which signifies a person who has a definite unique sense that shows itself through a strong willpower. The key words of this number are 'determination—uniqueness'. I find it interesting that Adam, the first name ever given to man, reveals exactly the qualities we would expect to come from the mythical first named man.

Analysing your first name is just scratching the surface. Once you begin to analyse your birth name and birthdate with a variety of simple calculations you gain a precise assessment of who you are, where your potential lies, where you are going, what your lessons and obstacles are and how to overcome them. (Lessons and obstacles are explained later on page 23.)

There is not one thing in our world and the universe that is not empowered by numbers and equations, with each human soul resonating to a particular and distinctive chord that can be defined using the science of numbers. Numerology deals with vibrations particular to the human soul. Each human being is unique and unlike anyone else.

Science has discovered the vibrations of light, colour, sound and electricity and has expressed the rate of these vibratory activities in numbers. Since the beginning of the twentieth century our knowledge of the physical world's number vibrations has greatly increased. Although the mind can neither fathom nor see an electron or an atom we must accept in faith the figures which science has given us. Musical notes are formulated by numbers; the higher the number the higher the frequency. Some people can see colours or auras around people, crystals, plants, which are a direct expression of energy vibrations.

There are both positive and negative energies in every number. The name delineations in this book are based upon the positive aspects the name offers. A person who is blocked or not in harmony with their vibrations is like a car whose engine is out of tune and not firing on all cylinders. This results in confusion and disharmony with energies scattered around and a broken or cloudy aura.

Inner awakenings occur when we begin to know and understand ourselves, an understanding which is of prime importance, yet how many of us feel comfortable with who we are and where we are going? Too few of us take time to think about these things or even act upon them. Numerology can reveal the answers to you, let you arrive at an understanding enabling you to grow and reach the true identity and pathway.

It is important to remember that numerology is not a means of fortune telling but an aid to foecasting and planning future events, taking your innate talents and abilities and the rhythms and cycles of life into account. When you understand life's rhythms and energy vibrations you can blend them together in harmony, using your inherent psychic abilities in a clear (and perhaps even clairvoyant) way. I use these energies when interpreting complete essence charts; I find them extremely effective in forecasting future events and cycles.

2   How to Use This Book

The 7000+ names in this book are listed alphabetically in the Index of Names and numerically in the Index of Numbers, which give the meanings attached to the numbers from 1 to 99 and names which bear those numbers.

Choosing a Name for a Child

You may wish to choose a child's name based on a particular character trait you would like the child to have. You would look up those attributes in the Index of Numbers and consider the names that correspond to them. This is discussed fully on page 32.

Although the Index of Names indicates a gender preference after each name it is important to realise that any name could be used for either sex as the interpretations are universal.

The names in the lists are generally used as first and middle names.

Analysing a Name

If you wish to analyse a name, look up the Index of Names (the alphabetical listing), find the name's number and then go to the interpretation of that number in the Index of Numbers (the numerical listing).

It is essential that the *full birth name* always be analysed first to determine the true vibrational energies that were brought into this life. Often a person is not living up to or working with the original energies they came to express. The birth name can be compared with an abbreviated or assumed name to see what strengths or weaknesses need to be dealt with.

Constructing Numerical Values

Surnames are not listed in the Index of Names, and some unusual given names may not be listed either. Such names are analysed by first establishing their numeric value according to the alpha-numeric conversion grid below. The master numbers 11 (for K) and 22 (for V) should always be shown and added as 11 and 22, not 1 + 1 or 2 + 2, for accurate interpretation. (Master numbers are explained on page 21.)

Titles such as Mr, Mrs, Miss, Ms, Her Majesty, Prince, Lord, President, Sister, Father, Brother, or any such salutation affixed to a name, should not be considered in the construction.

Alpha-Numeric Conversion Grid

1	2	3	4	5	6	7	8	9		11	22
A	B	C	D	E	F	G	H	I		K	V
J		L	M	N	O	P	Q	R			
S	T	U		W	X	Y	Z				

(Notice how K = 11; if reduced it would be a 2. V = 22, if reduced it would be a 4. It is important to recognise the value of the 11 and the 22 as master energies which are never reduced, as they divulge the detailed and accurate account of the total vibration.)

Name Construction Examples:

H   E   I   D   I

$$8 + 5 + 9 + 4 + 9 = 35$$

(go to 35 in the numerical listing for meaning)

G   I   R   V   A   N

$$7 + 9 + 9 + 22 + 1 + 5 = 53$$

(go to 53 in the numerical listing for meaning)

If a name results in a triple number it must be reduced to a double number to accurately reveal the vibration. This commonly happens when you calculate total names and pathways.

For example, 109 is treated as 10 and $9 = 10 + 9 = 19$.

Changing a Name

If you feel that you could enhance your character by changing your name to one which has attributes you would like in your life you should refer to the Index of Numbers. You must first analyse your birth name, however, as you cannot delete or get rid of birth name energies.

Total Names

Total names are more dynamic than single names, as they carry double and triple number vibrations. To find out what your total name means you look up your first name and your middle name, and construct your last name and any names not listed using the alpha-numeric conversion grid. The meanings are obtained from the Index of Numbers.

Example:

J O H N	W I N S T O N	L E N N O N
1+6+8+5	5+9+5+1+2+6+5	3+5+5+5+6+5
20 +	33	+ 29

John	20	Technical—Collaborator
Winston	33	Teacher—Counsellor
Lennon	29	Humanitarian—Way-shower
Total	82	Guide—Supportive A person with the energy vibration 82 is quietly powerful with high ideals, always ready to help others.

This chapter has given you a very brief overview of the elements of numerology—each topic is covered in depth in the following chapters.

3 Types of Numbers

In numerology we find four distinct types of numbers. The number type tells you how its meaning is achieved and/or felt.

1. Single numbers (1 to 9) reveal how the vibration is experienced or actually lived out.
2. Double and triple numbers (10 to 99 and 100 onwards) reveal subconscious knowledge.
3. Master numbers (11, 22, 33, 44, 55, 66, 77, 88, 99) reveal spiritual intelligence or wisdom.
4. Karmic numbers (13, 14, 16, 19) reveal lessons to overcome and learn.

Single Numbers

The single numbers 1 to 9 reveal how the number is experienced by its bearer.

Most people are familiar with the single numbers of numerology. However, after years of practice and research it became crystal clear to me that one could understand in more detail how a number is expressed by analysing the double number before reducing it to a single number.

For instance, analyse the double number 53 from the example shown on page 16 for the name Girvan; 53 means 'competitor, enterprising'.

A calculation which results in a single digit number reveals the outcome of that numeric vibration and how it would be experienced. To reach a single digit you simply add one number to the next until you reach a single digit. For example, 53 reduces to an 8 (5 + 3 = 8). As another example, the name Abe (A = 1) + (B = 2) + (E = 5) gives a total of 8. Because it is a single digit it is expressed as an experience.

The experience of an 8 is power, success and ambition. This information would most probably not be news to a person with this name, although they may not have been consciously aware of it. The power of 8 may not be used to its best advantage until 'Abe' acknowledges the energy force and works with it on a positive basis.

Double and Triple Numbers

The double and triple numbers (10 to 99 and 100 onwards) reveal subconscious knowledge brought into this life. In other words these energies exist in the mind, affecting behaviour and thought without entering the conscious awareness. This is what we do automatically, without thinking.

Most calculations add up to a double or triple number. Double numbers give a comprehensive meaning by *showing*, then *telling*, how a person reacts to the qualities of their name as it filters into the subconscious as information, thoughts and behaviours in their life. The interpretations 1 to 99 in the numerical listing were composed by taking into consideration the triple/double number, and the reduced single number experience.

All double and triple numbers are read from left to right, so that defining takes on a domino effect, the first number meaning blending in with the others until the outcome results in a total description.

A person with the number 73 is quite different to a person with the number 37. Although both reduce to 10, then to 1, the analysis process looks at which number is first as this predetermines where the emphasis begins and is automatically placed.

In the double number 37, the first number, 3, is associated with the meanings 'creative, charmer, self-expression, communication'. The emphasis is placed on the person being creative, charming, self-expressive and a communicator, so you would envisage an outgoing creative person.

The second number, which is a 7, tells how you enhance or refine the first number; it carries the meanings 'thinker, refined, perfectionist, quiet'.

The person would enhance the outgoing creative approach with perfection, thought and refinement.

The subconscious knowledge revealed by a 37 is 'trend-setter and communicator'. (These meanings are obtained from the Index of Numbers.) Compare this with a 73, the same numbers reversed. The 73 reveals this subconscious knowledge as a 'poetic, mystical person', quite unlike the qualities of a 37. What makes the difference is where the emphasis is first put. Remember this is automatic and in this case 7, the thinker, perfectionist, quiet and refined, is where the emphasis is placed first. This makes the person more reserved and quietly thoughtful. The second number, 3, is how they enhance the first number, which is through creativity, self-expression and communication. So the 37 is outgoing, creative with refined thinking, compared with the 73 who is a reserved, quiet thinker who creates and communicates from thought.

In the total number interpretation you must look at the other reduced numbers and the single number for assistance in determining the full meaning. For instance, both numbers in the above example reduce to a 10 (3 + 7 = 10) 'determined and unique', and then reduce to a 1 (1 + 0 = 1); the single number reveals how the vibration is experienced: 'independent, original, pioneer and leader'. Both numbers would experience their meanings in these ways.

This is all part of defining the total double number, and must be kept in mind as all numbers within a number have aspects that explain the final delineation.

If you have a triple number, e.g. 112, reduce it to a double number using the same method. Take the first two digits from the left (11) and add the last number (2) = 13. The two digits from the left show where the emphasis is placed, while the third number tells how the person refines or enhances the first two numbers. The resulting sum, 13, reveals how the subconscious knowledge will be filtered through. Then reduce to a single digit, 1 + 3 = 4, remembering to always check the double meanings first.

Most double and triple numbers when reduced still remain a double number. Before you reduce this to a single number to find out how the vibration will be experienced, check to see if the second double number is a karmic number or master number. If it is take it into consideration as either an obstacle to overcome (karmic number) or wisdom to use (master number) in experiencing the vibration. (Note: 14/5 is the correct format to record double to single number reductions; this is universally used to keep track of the original number. The correct format for recording numbers is 59/14/5, for example—the breakdown is 59 = 5 + 9 = 14 and 1 + 4 = 5.) (See page 23 for karmic numbers and below for master numbers.)

Numbers with a zero in the second and third positions give 10 and 100 times the power to the first number. You can understand this when you look at the value of money. If you have $100 it has more significance than $10, and $10 has more significance than $1. Numerology experiences the same effect—the more zeros the more power. The definition of a zero when combined with other numbers is 'wholeness, completion and allness'—it magnifies the value of the first number.

It is not essential to go into such detail when researching your numbers as the listings from 1 to 99 do that step for you; however, for the serious student it can be of benefit for a deeper understanding of numerology.

Master Numbers

The master numbers 11, 22, 33, 44, 55, 66, 77, 88 and 99 reveal the spiritual wisdom contained in a name or meaning.

As you no doubt noticed, these numbers are all doubles of the same number. Being double numbers they are interpreted as a whole number first, with the meaning expressed as energy vibrations of a spiritual nature or as wisdom from a higher source.

Most numerologists only explain and interpret the master numbers 11, 22 and 33, believing these to be the 'highest' master numbers possible. However, all master numbers 11 through to 99 reveal a potential for growth and understanding once their bearers become awakened to using this higher spiritual information.

From my research on master numbers it appears that very few people actually live up to their higher potential; instead they end up becoming irritated with the world as a sense of frustration overwhelms them. (People with master numbers are frequently extremely sensitive and highly strung with eccentric and/or erratic behaviour which is hard to understand.)

If you have master number vibrations in your chart, but the focus of your life revolves around earthly and egotistic energies, you are most probably working on the single vibration, for example on a 2 instead of an 11. If your thoughts revolve on philosophical and/or metaphysical concepts you are operating at the master number level. Master numbers 77 and 88 reduce to the karmic numbers 14 and 16; this gives a challenge as these vibrations can have a tendency to get stuck in the karmic lesson instead of allowing the spiritual wisdom to flow through. (See karmic lessons, page 24.)

Often the qualities of master numbers come through as intuition, as feelings of knowingness or as guidance from beyond. Some people may feel lucky and gifted. The master numbers are gifts which carry with them a duty to fulfil an obligation or goal. Their qualities are particularly meaningful as they are the intensified interpretation of the one number, with the first digit showing where emphasis is placed and the second digit telling how the first one is enhanced. Since master numbers have the same number in both positions its power is enhanced and therefore the meaning deepened. A large master number does not mean a person is better or wiser, it only illustrates the type of wisdom that can be utilised.

Some people who choose to use a shortened or abbreviated version of their name may be missing the spiritual vibration of a master number. For years I used the shortened name Laure (21); only when I became aware of the master energies of my given name, Laureli (33), was I able to tune in and utilise the spiritual wisdom with positive results.

Comparison of the full name Thomas with the short name Tom

Thomas = 22/4 The 22 master energy reveals spiritual wisdom; builder, balance and strength. The single number 4 shows the actual experience; organised, practical, hardworking and disciplined.

Tom = 12/3 The double number 12 reveals the subconscious knowledge of a crusader and genial person. The single number 3 shows the actual experience as creative, charmer, expressive communicator.

It is dangerous for the bearers of master numbers to become egotistical, to believe that they are more 'spiritual' or 'better' than someone without master numbers, as the energies involved can be difficult to live up to. It is important to understand that a person would not have brought master number vibrations (or any vibrations) into their life if they could not live up to or handle them. It may not be easy but the rewards for achievement and growth are well worth the efforts made and the hardships overcome.

Master Numbers and their Single Digit Counterparts:

11/2 22/4 33/6 44/8 55/10/1 66/12/3 77/14/5
88/16/7 99/18/9

See the numerical listing for character analysis of the master numbers.

Karmic Numbers

The Karmic numbers 13, 14, 16, 19 reveal the lessons to be learned and/or overcome.

Karma is a Sanskrit word meaning simply 'deed' or 'action'. Karma is an important concept in both Buddhism and Hinduism, according to which a person's status in life is determined by their deeds in a previous state of existence, and their fate in the next life determined by actions in this life.

Karma is referred to as the law of cause and effect. In numerology karma shows itself in the form of a circumstance or situation that we are experiencing that we must recognise and overcome. Karma repeats itself over and over again in the guise of different, although similar, situations or as people who though outwardly different are very much the same. Karmic happenings are there for us to conquer or overcome so we can get on with our job of being ourselves. It is thought these obstacles are brought into our lives because in past lives we either abused or neglected the thing we are to come to terms with, or perhaps we were faced with the same karmic lesson which we did not master and so must try again. Karma is not impossible to overcome, but it requires awareness, discipline and patience. Most people experience karma in one form or another. Karmic experience actually enables a person to learn and grow; it is not a handicap, nor is it impossible to overcome.

The karmic number 13 reveals that the person is to work hard and do their fair share in life, be stable and forthright in dealings with other people. This comes from past abuses of burdening other people and being lazy and superficial or just skimming by.

The karmic number 14 shows that the person needs to learn from experience, to quit making the same mistakes and to try to work with difficulties instead of running away from them. This karmic situation comes from past destructive and erratic behaviour, often from over-indulgence in the physical sense, especially alcohol, sex and gambling.

The karmic number 16 indicates a person who is overly self-concerned and introverted; they come across as diffident and often unapproachable. The 16 should try to be more open and understanding of the world but instead they often draw to themselves misfortunes and strange happenings which cause them to retreat even further.

The karmic number 19 comes from past abuse of power for self-fulfilment. These people often do not even realise that they are completely self-absorbed. Unlike the 16, the 19 is normally extroverted and egotistical. They can become dependent and meet with many obstacles until they work towards balancing their needs with others' needs.

Karmic lessons Karma is indicated in another important way as well as by the four numbers. A person's full birth name may not contain all the numbers from 1 to 9. The missing numbers indicate what particular energies that person needs to work on and/or overcome to be more balanced. These are referred to as karmic lessons.

The meaning is the negative aspect of the missing number. As the person matures they become points in life that are often consciously worked on, the person feeling compelled to overcome or correct them as they are put in positions where their life would be simpler if they developed these vibrations. For the purpose of determining which numbers are missing, count the K as 2 and the V as 4—this is the only area in a chart where these letters are used in their single number values.

People often are missing several numbers but it does not mean anything more than that they have several lessons to learn. They usually have very colourful lives with many interesting experiences and challenges.

Having all the numbers represented in a name doesn't necessarily leave room for complacency; it can make the person seem balanced with few challenges. They often feel unmotivated and find it hard to commit to anything. No matter if you are missing numbers or not, your name is exactly what you require to be you.

Example of No Missing Numbers
(*Note the K is looked at as a 2 when checking for missing numbers.)

M I C H A E L   J O S E P H
4 + 9 + 3 + 8 + 1 + 5 + 3   1 + 6 + 1 + 5 + 7 + 8
        33   +   28

            J A C K* S O N
            1 + 1 + 3 + 11/2 + 1 + 6 + 5
                    28

Total name of 89 = Advisor—Motivator. (The total 89 is calculated with the K = 11 but note it is recorded as 11/2 in the chart as a reminder when looking for missing numbers that 2 is counted.) The recorded total would be: 89/17/8.

Example Missing Two Numbers (no 2s or 7s)

J O H N   M A R W O O D   C L E E S E
1+6+8+5   4+1+9+5+6+6+4   3+3+5+5+1+5

    20   +   35   +   22

Total for name of 77 = Master energy vibration, restorer—unconventional. When reduced (77/14/5) becomes a 14, which brings the person the karmic challenges to overcome before they can experience the energy of the master vibration.

Missing 2: There is no B, K or T in the given name. This indicates a need to be detailed, supportive, cooperative and balanced. There may be a tendency to go overboard, with too much or not enough detail or cooperation. (Note: This is the negative aspect of a 2. See Index of Numbers for meanings.)

Continued on page 26

> **Missing 7:** There is no G, P or Y in the given name. This indicates there is a need to take time to think, to perfect things and have tranquillity and quiet time alone. The person may become quite moody and too much of a perfectionist, being extremely hard to please. (The negative aspects of a 7.)
>
> Although the total name sums a 77 it does not deflect from the missing 7. Instead it means the person cannot escape the effects of the missing 7, as the double number 77 reveals the subconscious and automatic thoughts which magnify the missing 7, making the person acutely aware of a problem to overcome.

A helpful way to conquer these karmic lessons (missing numbers) is to add all the missing numbers from the name together and reduce them to a single digit. This gives you an indication of how to overcome the lessons of the missing numbers by applying that single number positively. In John Cleese, for example, 2 + 7 = 9. The total karmic lesson is a 9 indicating that he should be compassionate, more of a humanitarian, and complete projects.

It is common for a person to be missing a number and have it appear as one of their main numbers in their chart somewhere else. It emphasises or exaggerates the negative aspects as a flaw for the person to be consciously aware of to overcome.

Birth Path Numbers

A complete numerology chart includes a person's birth path and pathway. To obtain these energies you must first determine the birth path number.

Birth path numbers are given by the total of the birth date. It shows the opportunities present from birth that a person can use to express themselves. Often numerologists look at the birth path as the vibration that describes the attributes of the type of career a person can successfully undertake. The birth path is the road or path that is set and unchangeable for the person to take and complements the wisdom and experience from the total birth name.

The birth path is calculated by simply adding together the numbers of the birth date, then reducing them to a single number. This is similar to

Table of Birth Path Meanings

1 Leadership or executive qualities often resulting in self-employment.

2 Assistant or aide, behind-the-scenes person. Detailed and precise.

3 Skilled craftsman, often in arts. Communicator and social.

4 The worker, often hard labourer. Works well with hands, likes to build.

5 The explorer, very versatile. Jack of all trades. A developer.

6 The provider. Enjoys health and healing; involved with social issues.

7 Analytical. Interested in history and literature. Drawn to mysticism.

8 The manager. Good in corporate affairs. Loves competition.

9 A philanthropist. Drawn to healing and counselling. Good politician.

working with name numbers, but the meanings of the single numbers are defined differently as shown in the table of birth path meanings.

As an example: John Cleese was born October 27th, 1939 or 10–27–1939. (In numerology you always work with the sequence month, day, year.)

The birth date format would look like this:

$$1 + 0 + 2 + 7 + 1 + 9 + 3 + 9 = 32.$$

Reduced to a single digit, $3 + 2 = 5$. Birth paths are defined in single number meanings. The number 5 carries the meaning: 'The explorer, very versatile. A developer, jack of all trades.' It is helpful to look at the meaning of a 32 in the numerical listing to see how the number is subconsciously felt, as this will give you suggestions as to what kind of opportunities may be expressed.

Pathway

The pathway or purpose in life is what we quite often jokingly refer to as the 'map' we wish we were born with. Numerology gives us this look at what we are here to do using our 'birth blueprint'.

The pathway is not normally consciously realised until a person is more mature and approximately 45 to 58 years old. Often people are side-tracked and until something triggers them into the pursuit of their purpose they find their life's true meaning and fulfilment elusive. Triggers are found in a variety of occurrences including near death experiences, the ending of a relationship (either through death or divorce or argument), the birth of a child, a major unheaval in life—the list is endless.

To calculate the pathway you must work with the original birth name and the birth path, adding the name total to the two-digit total of the

Table of Pathway Meanings

1   To create your own individuality without being directed by or separated from others. To be happy with yourself, feeling whole and complete.

2   To be a peacemaker, first with yourself. Others will look to you as mediator and diplomat. To be a firm and kind and good judge of people and situations.

3   Share talents with others using inner creativity with self-expression. Often held back by lack of self-esteem. There is much to offer and much to achieve once allowed.

4   Establish perseverance with patience. Becoming a solid beacon, honest and trustworthy. Must guard against becoming set in ways and rigid.

5   To bring progress and change into the world with harmony for the good of humanity. The entrepreneurs of the world.

6   To be of service and help others without taking on their responsibilities. Teach others how to do for themselves. Learn to let go, cut the apron strings. Give unconditional love.

7   To search from within using intuition. Be a philosopher, reflective, healer and teacher.

8   To balance the physical nature with the spiritual self. To give and receive in balanced measure. Until this is maintained, people and things in life come and go, there is no stability.

9   To be selfless in tolerance and compassionate to all. To embrace and become the healer or teacher or mentor you came to be.

birth path and reducing them to a single number. The pathway meanings are again different and defined on the previous page.

On page 17 we constructed the numerology name chart for John Lennon, so we can add to this his birth path to find his pathway.

John Winston Lennon, born October 9th, 1940

(For simplicity you can drop the zeros if you like.)

$1 + 9 + 1 + 9 + 4 = 24$

Total name	= 82 Integrity—supportive
Birth path	= 24 (2 + 4 = 6; see 6 in the table of birth path meanings.)
Thus, birth path	6 The provider; enjoys health and healing; involved with social issues

Adding name total to two-digit birth path (82 + 24)

Total for pathway	= 106 (reduce to 10 + 6 = 16, then to 1 + 6 = 7)
Thus, pathway	= 7 Search from within using intuition; a philosopher, reflective, healer and teacher. (See 7 in table of pathway meanings.)

4 Understanding a Name

A name can be likened to a vehicle or tool which we have brought into this life from accumulated experiences in previous lifetimes which enables us to travel at our own speed, in our own unique manner, cultivating our talents and abilities as we go. Often, however, people do not live up to or work with the energies that they originally came to express and only resonate to a lower or negative vibration. This is rather like riding a bicycle when you have a shiny new car available.

As defined in *Webster's 20th Century Unabridged Dictionary* a name is 'a word or phrase by which a person, thing or class of thing is known, called or spoken to, or of; an appellation; a title'. It is our identity. Using the numerology name delineations you can come to a realisation of your true talents and abilities.

It is important to analyse a person's full birth name to determine the true vibrational energies that person has, which will reveal talents, abilities, strengths, weaknesses and lessons. When a person uses an abbreviated form of their name or perhaps a totally different name it can alter how they perceive themselves and how they operate. Different spellings of the same name bring different perceptions also, as the example on the next page demonstrates.

> **Abbreviated name, full name:**
> TONY = 20 Technical—collaborator   *versus*
> ANTHONY = 34 Intuition—technical
> Both names are technical with Tony having collaborator skills,
> working jointly with others. Anthony has intuition talents and
> abilities available that are enhanced by technical attributes.
>
> **Same name, different spelling, and abbreviation:**
> STEVEN = 40 Solid—rational   *versus*
> STEPHEN = 33 Teacher —counsellor
> *Abbreviated:* STEVE = 35 Ambitious—resourceful
> Steven would be security conscious and self-motivated; Stephen,
> spiritually minded and a creative communicator; Steve, a creative
> risk-taker, open to the new.

Discovering such different energy outcomes just illustrates how the
realisation of their true traits can help someone. The birth name is the
essential starting place as it alone gives us an honest and accurate account
of potentials and who we are or could be.

Different Types of Names

We are complex beings made up of many energy vibrations. Each of our
names provides a vibration. Most people have at least three names, some
more, some less. To deepen our understanding of the total name and how
it functions it is important to know what each name represents.

In our charting we will be breaking down the names into 6 categories:
first name, *middle* name, *last* name, *total* name, *vowels* and *consonants*.

Some cultures and people name their children with several names,
sometimes up to eight different names or possibly more. To determine
which category the multiple name belongs to and how to handle it you
should use the following basic rules of thumb. The person for whom the
chart is being prepared may be able to help you determine where the name
belongs (first names, middle names and last names). If that is not possible
then use the obvious choices.

For example, Mary Elizabeth Josephine Antoinette Miller is the birth name. If the person used Mary Elizabeth as her first name then Josephine Antoinette would be her middle name and Miller the last name. But what if she considered that Mary was her true first name? Mary would be considered the first name, Elizabeth Josephine Antoinette the middle name and Miller the last name.

Members of the British Royal family have up to six given names. The five middle names would be added up as one excessively long name. This may account for some of their seemingly confused behaviour.

If you should use more than one name, with or without a hyphen, it is recognised as the full name, e.g. Debra Lee, Mary Louise, Morgan-Leigh, Heron-Blyth or Soria-Garcia. Often a person with a hyphenated name will have no middle name. If in doubt do an analysis using both names as the first name and a comparison dividing the names, one as first and one as the middle. The energy vibrations that appear may be your guide as to where the names fit.

Multiple last names should be added as one total for a true category type analysis.

First Name

The first name is the *key to the character*. It is the personal and physical side to how you perceive and carry yourself.

Middle Name

The middle name or *inner secret self* shows as emotions. It is the part of the character that sets the tone for how one reacts to situations.

Having no middle name at all often means that a person has a difficult time expressing emotion. Such a person may appear strong and secure on the outside while inside they are in turmoil, or they may find it hard to express emotions and be overly emotional with frequent outbursts. People without middle names must learn to balance their emotions; unbalanced emotions can result in frustration not only for themselves but for those around them.

Last Name

The last name (family name, surname) represents how you seize life and use your intellect to navigate your way through life. This is referred to as the *contemplative self*. Some numerologists believe the last name is where you reveal your hereditary characteristics, either passed on via genes or as a direct result of conditioning as a child. Regardless of where it comes from it drives your thinking process.

Often people change or add to their last name through marriage. For a correct analysis you should do a chart of your full birth name and compare it with any changes which the 'new' name brings into your comprehension.

Total Name

The total name, which is the sum of all a person's names, reveals the *true identity*, which is the combination of the key to the character (first name), the inner secret self (middle name), and the contemplative facility (the last name). It shows how you understand and grasp the use of the accumulated experiences of past lives that are brought through this vibration.

Women who have changed their name by marriage must go back to their birth name for an accurate reading. Let's take Jacqueline Onassis as an example; she was born:

$$
\begin{array}{ll}
\text{J A C Q U E L I N E} & \text{L E E} \\
1+1+3+8+3+5+3+9+5+5 & 3+5+5 \\
\qquad\qquad 43 \qquad\qquad + & \qquad 13 \\
\text{B O U V I E R} & \\
2+6+3+22+9+5+9 & \\
+ \qquad 56 &
\end{array}
$$

First name JACQUELINE
  = 43   Researcher—secretive   *Key to character*

Middle name LEE
  = 13   Transformer—disciplined   *Inner secret self*

Last name BOUVIER
    = 56   Ambassador—judge   *Contemplative self*

Total name
    = 112   Reduce to 11 + 2 = 13
                Transformer—disciplined   *True identity*

From what we know about this person we would believe that this is an accurate analysis. It is interesting to note that her *true identity* (total name) and her *inner secret self* (middle name) have the same vibration. This duality shows that these two areas are strong forces in her life, especially as 13 is also a karmic number which brings added challenges to overcome first.

People who do not use their full names must do calculations based on their birth name for accuracy.

See pages 39–41 for how to analyse name changes.

Vowels and Consonants

In school you learned about vowels and consonants. They are speech sounds from which all words and names are formed. In numerology they specify certain aspects of a person for a complete delineation.

Vowels

Vowels reveal the inner disposition or *individualism*. The vowel value can be likened to the inner motor that drives and compels a person to be an individual, separate and different. Think of it as your individu-vowel-ity. In numerology A, E, I, O, U and often Y are vowels.

The following guide will assist you to determine the use of Y.

1. Y is a vowel when it makes a vowel sound like ee, e.g. Gary, Mary, Johnny.
2. Y is a vowel when it follows another vowel and is sounded as one, e.g. ay as in May, Wayne, Gaye.

3. Y is a vowel when there is no other vowel in the syllable, e.g. Harry, Tony.
4. Y is a consonant when it makes the sound as in yet and yes, e.g. Yale, Young, Lanyon.

Most of the time the Y is considered a vowel, but always check the guidelines for assistance.

Consonants

Consonants reveal the *personality*. This can be likened to a mask, not necessarily a true picture of the character; however, it is how people describe you as this is what you show to others. People often find it difficult to distinguish between who they mask (consonants) and who they are (vowels). Think of it as who we *con* the world into thinking we are (con, short for consonants).

When constructing a chart we reflect the consonants on the top of the letters of the name and the vowels under the letters, with the totals on the bottom.

Example

```
4       9           2   8       Consonants = 23 Personality
D   O   R   O   T   H   Y
    6       6           7       Vowels = 20 Individuality
          4 3                   Total = 43 True identity
```

To recap what we have learned so far, let's look at a famous President of the United States, John Quincy Adams, born July 11th, 1767. He was very influential in diplomatic affairs and foreign relations. He lived from 1767 to 1848 and was nicked named 'Old Man Eloquent' by his peers. This gentleman was far beyond his time with his far-seeing and far-reaching ideals.

Birth path: $7+11+1+7+6+7=39$ $(3+9=12)$ $1+2=3$.   Record 39/12/3.

Notice that the 11 was not reduced when adding the birth path as it is one of the master numbers, which are never reduced during this process.

```
1   8 5   8    5 3      4     4 1  = 39 Consonants
J O H N   Q U I N C Y  A D A M S
  6        3 9      7 1    1      = 27 Vowels
   20    +    35    +    11       = 66 Total
```

If the three names had not added up to the same total as the vowels and consonants, the calculation would have been wrong. This is a good way to double check your addition.

e.g. John (20) + Quincy (35) + Adams (11) equals the total name (66).

The consonants (39) + the vowels (27) equals the total name (66).

First name: John
  = 20   Technical—collaborator   *Key to character*
Middle name: Quincy
  = 35   Ambitious—resourceful   *Inner secret self*
Last name: Adams
  = 11   Visionary—charismatic   *Contemplative self*
Consonants
  = 39   Composed—discriminating   *Personality*
Vowels
  = 27   Peaceful—devoted   *Individualism*
Total name
  = 66   Healer—uplifter   *True identity*
Birth path
  = 39/12/3   Skilled craftsman,
                  communicator   *Path or route*
Pathway or purpose
  = 105/15/6   Provider, involved
(total name + birth path)   with social issues *Purpose*
Missing number
  = no 2s   Details, cooperation, supportive and balance

The information derived from these nine areas provides us with an accurate analysis of this person. History provides us with detailed information for comparison—see next page.

Key to character (20): A devoted man, Adams was very resourceful with worldwide associations.

Inner secret self (35): His emotional side could be explosive yet with his resourceful inner self he would use it to his advantage.

Contemplative self (11): Able to think and see ahead of his time and draw the right like-minded people to him.

Personality (39): A sociable person, he could handle all types of people and situations with discrimination.

Individualism (27): Once committed to an idea or principle he would never walk away without trying his best.

True identity (66): The master vibration of his total name gave him the ability to bring peace, and heal what was around him with understanding, uplifting others.

Birth path (3): Eloquent with words (he was fluent in at least five languages), and a great orator, he wrote several famous papers.

Pathway (6): Involved in politics and community affairs all his life, he served as Secretary of State, with many ministerial positions, finally becoming the sixth President of the United States.

Karmic lesson (no 2s): He had to become adept at handling details and cooperative associations.

5 Changing a Name

Often people consult a numerologist for advice on altering their names in the hope that the change will improve their lives. In my experience, however, people are often not aware of the potential within the names they already have. It is important to take time to identify and understand the energies a person already carries before undertaking a name change; a name change may otherwise cause chaos to reign until the true talents, abilities and perhaps lessons are first dealt with. Again, you must always work with the full birth name.

Once the true energies have been identified it may be possible to successfully alter a name to be consistent with the person's natural strengths and weaknesses and thus create more harmony in their lives.

Marriage

The most common reason for a name change is marriage. Earlier we looked at the total birth name of Jacqueline Onassis (Jacqueline Lee Bouvier). Her total birth name (true identity) was a 13 (transformer —disciplined).

Let's see how the name change to Kennedy, the contemplative self, affected her new identity (total name).

```
K   E   N   N   E   D   Y
11+5 + 5 + 5 + 5 + 4 + 7    = 42  Contemplative self
                                  Emotional—traditional


Total name becomes: Jacqueline = 43
                           Lee = 13
                       Kennedy = 42
New identity                     98  Subtle—proficient
```

The last name would have brought her contemplative self into traditional and emotional thinking, with her new identity (total name) lending subtle tones and proficiency to all she undertook. The general public took her to their hearts and she became a role model for millions of people around the world.

How did the name change in the contemplative self affect her identity when she became Onassis?

```
O   N   A   S   S   I   S
6 + 5 + 1 + 1 + 1 + 9 + 1    = 24  Contemplative self
                                   Parental—giver


Total name becomes: Jacqueline = 43
                           Lee = 13
                       Onassis = 24
New identity                     80  Prosperous—self-reliant
```

Interestingly, history tells us that she married Onassis as a means of protection for herself and her children as well as for financial security. The contemplative or thinking nature became focused on being parental and giving, with her new identity aiming for prosperity and self-reliance.

Guidelines for Name Changes

The following guidelines are useful in helping to determine what you could change your name to.

1. Make a list of the attributes you would like to have that are missing in your birth name and birth path, e.g. compassion, balance, composure, power, self-control, wealth, friends.
2. List your talents, abilities, shortcomings and challenges honestly.
3. Consider whether you are truly utilising the energy vibrations you have from your birth name and birth path.
4. Do complete calculations incorporating all the name changes you are considering to see what the results would be.

If in doubt consult a numerologist for guidance and information on the best time to activate a name change.

Remember that you can never delete or get rid of the energies of your birth name, although you can add to them with a name change, often with good results if you are aware of what energies you are working with.

Adoption

What if you were adopted?

From time to time I am consulted by people who have been adopted and are distressed to learn they were given at birth a name different from the one their adoptive parents gave them. After extensive study and research I have come to the conclusion that although it is important to analyse both sets of names, the name the person thought was theirs on a conscious level in this case has more emphasis. Sometimes we come into the world through people we don't even know. It is our way of reaching certain groups of people and situations we could not have encountered in the normal way. Generally the first naming reflects a temporary energy emanating from the birth parents and reveals more of their emotional state than the real vibrations the child has come to complete.

People who require more information or guidance are advised to see a professional numerologist.

Naming a Child

Most numerologists believe there are no coincidences and that the names we are given at birth are intuitively inspired by invisible helpers and divine messengers. These inspirations influence the namer as the spirit coming into this incarnation resonates to its own distinctive chord which requires its own special map. This helps to explain the fact that the names given in addition to hereditary last names represent a true analysis of a person's character energy vibrations.

It is very helpful to let the incoming child send you information on what type of person it will be. This information comes through as feelings and thoughts to the namer. You can then make a list of attributes you believe the child may have and go to the numerical listing for a favourable name from meanings that match. I do not feel that we should try to force any name on a child, but let the true name come through. This has been working since the beginning of time, as the incoming soul knows best how to communicate with the right people. If you have blocks, I suggest you relax and let it be until the right name comes to you.

I am often asked to assist expectant parents. It is important to understand that we adults are acting as messengers to enable the unborn person to find their true name. Recently one parent came up with two names that were similar sounding but were spelt differently. The mother liked the look of one name but kept coming back to the alternative spelling. Of course the two names had different interpretations. The name she preferred was for a person who would be refined, scholarly, a quiet achiever. The day the child was born she said she just couldn't get the alternative name out of her mind and felt compelled to name the child with that selection, a name for a more vocal, aggressive person. She tells me it fits her child exactly.

6 Name Numerology Charts

Worked Example

As a review we will do a full name numerology chart on Steven Spielberg, born December 18th, 1947.

Birth path calculation: $1 + 2 + 1 + 8 + 1 + 9 + 4 + 7 = 33$ $(3 + 3) = 6$. Note the master energy that comes with this birth path reveals spiritual wisdom. See numeric listing for definition of a 33.

```
1 2  22   5  + 1 7    3 2    9 7  Consonants = 59
S T E V E N    S P I E L B E R G
   5    5    +      9 5      5    Vowels  = 29/11
      40               48         Total   = 88/16/7
```

Continues on next page

First name Steven
= 40	Solid—rational	*Key to character*

Last name Spielberg
= 48	Astute—achiever	*Contemplative self*

Consonants
= 59	Methodical—explorer	*Personality*

Vowels
= 29	Teacher—humanitarian	*Individuality*

Total name
= 88	Crusader—perfectionist	*True identity*

Birth path
= 33/6	Provider, involved with social issues	*Path or route*

Pathway
= 121/13/4	Perseverance, solid, honest	*Purpose*

Missing numbers
= 6	Responsibility, home, family love	*Karmic lesson*
= 8	Power, success, ambition, authority	*Karmic lesson*

Total karmic lessons
= 14	Detached—impulsive

Note: Mr Spielberg has no middle name. As you can see, it has not held him back, but it does mean that his inner self or emotions require a conscious effort to keep balanced.

The total name is a master number (88), which reveals spiritual wisdom through the true identity as a crusader and perfectionist, giving the potential of being highly strung. This vibration when reduced becomes the karmic number 16 (overly self-concerned, introverted, unapproachable and different). He would have had to overcome this in order to achieve what he has to date. His pathway (13) reveals karma before it is reduced to a 4; this shows his route or path has challenges as he perseveres to be solid; he could get carried away with transforming things and must use discipline (13) in order to keep on track.

By analysing all the aspects of Mr Spielberg's character from the chart information we can discover his true abilities and talents, his potentials and his weaknesses. This type of information would be very helpful to any psychoanalyst were they inclined to use it.

The blank chart on pages 46-47 has been prepared for you to calculate your own chart or anyone else's you are curious about. Feel free to make copies of this chart as it will assist you in your pursuit of understanding.

Should you have any questions or comments about this book, you can write to me at The Blyth Centre, PO Box 796, Burwood NSW 2134 Australia. Personal numerology charts with taped readings are available by mail or in person.

Name Numerology Chart

	1	2	3	4	5	6	7	8	9		11	22
Alpha-Numeric	A	B	C	D	E	F	G	H	I		K	V
Conversion												
Grid	J		L	M	N	O	P	Q	R			
	S	T	U	.	W	X	Y	Z				

Full birth certificate name:..

Birth date:...

Birth path calculation .... + ... + ... = ...
                              MONTH   DAY   YEAR   TOTAL

Birth Name Calculation

.... + ... + ... consonants = ...

.... + ... + ...
FIRST NAME   MIDDLE NAME   LAST NAME

.... + ... + ... vowels = ...

.... Total = ...
FIRST NAME   MIDDLE NAME   LAST NAME
TOTAL   TOTAL   TOTAL

Definition

First name	=	....	....	*Key to character*
Middle name	....	=	....	*Inner secret self*
Last name	=	....	....	*Contemplative self*
Consonants..........	=	....	....	*Personality*
Vowels	=	....	....	*Individuality*
Total name	=	....	....	*True identity*

Birth path	....	=	....	*Path or route*
Pathway	....	=	....	*Purpose*
Missing numbers	....	=	....	*Karmic lesson*
	....	=	....	*Karmic lesson*
Total karmic numbers	....	=	....	*Karmic lesson*

Master numbers to consider:...

Spiritual wisdom areas:...

Karmic numbers and lessons:..

Lesson areas:...

Name change:..

			Definition	Category
New name	....	=	....	....
New name	....	=	....	....
New name	....	=	....	....
New total	....	=	....	*Contemplative self*

Notes: ....

....

....

....

....

....

....

Prepared by:... Date:......................

Key Word Meanings for the Numbers 1–9

Listed below are the key word meanings for the nine single digit numbers. The double digit numbers in each category are included to illustrate how each number from 10 to 99 reduces to a single number.

1
PIONEER, LEADER, LONER, ORIGINAL
1 10 19 28 37 46 55 64 73 82 91

2
COOPERATIVE, DETAILED, BALANCED
2 11 20 29 38 47 56 65 74 83 92

3
CREATIVE, JOY, SOCIAL, COMMUNICATION
3 12 21 30 39 48 57 66 75 84 93

4
WORKER, ORGANISER, LOGICAL, REGIMENT
4 13 22 31 40 49 58 67 76 85 94

5
MOVER, FREEDOM, TRAVEL, CHANGE
5 14 23 32 41 50 59 68 77 86 95

6
HOME, FAMILY, NURTURER, RESPONSIBLE
6 15 24 33 42 51 60 69 78 87 96

7
THINKER, LONER, PERFECTIONIST, QUIET
7 16 25 34 43 52 61 70 79 88 97

8
ACHIEVER, COMPETITIVE, AMBITIOUS
8 17 26 35 44 53 62 71 80 89 98

9
HUMANITARIAN, COMPLETION, IDEALISTIC
9 18 27 36 45 54 63 72 81 90 99

7 Index of Numbers

Meanings for the Numbers 1 to 99

1
INDEPENDENT ORIGINAL PIONEER LEADER

A self-reliant person with strong leadership qualities. An original thinker who appears strong-minded; an ideas person.

2
DETAILED COOPERATIVE SUPPORTIVE BALANCED

A person who enjoys detailed work. Patient, tolerant and quick to please. Tries to maintain balance and harmony in all situations.

3
CREATIVE CHARMER EXPRESSIVE COMMUNICATOR

A person with a versatile flair for creating. Can be shy when young. Must take care not to become scattered. Excellent at communication in oral or written skills. Great salesperson.

Asa

4
ORGANISED PRACTICAL HARDWORKER DISCIPLINED
A serious and structured person. Approaches life in a practical way; often thought of as down-to-earth.

5
CAREFREE CURIOUS FREEDOM CHANGE
A carefree, happy-go-lucky type ruled by the five senses. Curious by nature, always ready for a new experience.

Asta	Sal	Tab	Tu

6
RESPONSIBLE HONEST LOVE HOME & FAMILY
A person who is honest and trustworthy. Has a tendency to take on responsibility without thinking of the consequences.

Abba	Ada	Babs	Bassa	Sam
Abu	Baba	Bal		

7
THINKER REFINED PERFECTIONIST QUIET
An observant person who enjoys contemplative pursuits. Often thought of as dignified and reserved. Looks for perfection in all situations and people.

Abbas	Ana	Dat	Mab	Ula
Alba	Bala	Jan	Maja	

8
POWER & SUCCESS AMBITION AUTHORITY
GIVE & RECEIVE
This person can be extremely competitive with a desire to have power and to succeed. The key is giving and receiving in balanced measure.

Abe	El	Laus	Sax	Uma
Amasa	Jana	Mac	Sula	Utu
Amat	Jans	Mata	Sy	Wat
Amba	Jud	Nu	Tama	Wu
Bea	Lala	Saul	Uda	

9
COMPASSION WISE HUMANITARIAN COMPLETION

A person with high ideals who feels for others and responds in considerate compassionate ways. Seem wiser than their years. Compelled to complete projects.

Ace	Bess	Job	Nata	Tana
Adal	Bud	Lan	Salus	Tess
Ajax	Cuc	Lea	Saula	Una
Alam	Dusa	Luba	Seba	Wal
Alda	Esta	Luc	Stan	
Alma	Fu	Matt	Sue	
Amata	Jay	Musa	Sun	

10
DETERMINED UNIQUE

This person will have a definite unique sense that will show itself through strong will-power.

Adam	Ebba	Jed	Oata	Tsao
Alan	Eda	Joab	Ola	Ulla
Anata	Elsa	Juan	Salma	Ute
Ash	Ema	Jubal	Santa	Watt
Baum	Esau	Judas	Stana	Yu
Beta	Etta	Lana	Tamba	
Bob	Jace	Luca	Tatam	
Dan	Jael	Mae	Tate	
Dea	Jamal	Nala	Tessa	

11
VISIONARY CHARISMATIC

A Master vibration that gives an ability to know and see beyond the visible. People are naturally drawn to this person; a natural charmer.

Abel	Beau	Ena	Max	Teata
Abessa	Bela	Ewa	Naatja	Ted
Adama	Calca	Hu	Nada	Wan
Adan	Calla	Isa	Nama	
Alana	Cate	Jade	Nan	
Amama	Claus	Jai	Oma	
Ane	Cle	Janus	Sade	
Ann	Dana	Jen	Samala	
Asha	Deb	Jesus	Susan	
Beal	Dula	Lucas	Tadd	

12
INVENTIVE CRUSADER

A leader with high ideals and a keen mind to solve problems. Can appear restless, with nervous energies. Enjoys socialising.

Abby	Cale	Jane	Mate	Sean
Agata	Cato	Jann	Maud	Sena
Alban	Clan	Jean	May	Syd
Alec	Clea	Jens	Mel	Tai
Aleta	Coba	Joe	Meta	Tatum
Alun	Col	Jon	Nana	Tom
Alys	Dag	Judd	Natal	Tulla
Amos	Elata	Laban	Ona	Ulf
Amy	Ella	Lace	Paca	Walta
Anna	Eos	Lael	Raja	Yma
Antal	Gad	Lajos	Sapta	Zac
Ayla	Hal	Leal	Sara	
Bee	Ita	Li	Sasha	
Ben	James	Lou	Satya	
Blase	Janda	Lulu	Scot	

13
TRANSFORMER DISCIPLINED

A karmic vibration that requires the person to be orderly and disciplined. Often such a person is either a workaholic or extremely lazy until they learn to transform and balance in a creative way.

Abbot	Cesca	Jose	Luana	Tane
Abdul	Cola	Jude	Lute	Tara
Afan	Dale	Jules	Maya	Tasha
Ali	Dallas	Junus	Muna	Teuta
Allan	Daya	Jye	Nuala	Toma
Ante	Elma	Kaj	Pan	Tsai
Ascot	Este	Lame	Patu	Tzu
Assar	Hala	Leala	Rata	Ubald
Bara	Ila	Leda	Sefa	Usha
Blue	Jacob	Lee	Sita	Yama
Budd	Jesse	Lew	Star	Yul
Buto	Joan	Lis	Sten	
Catana	Jocasa	Lola	Tacy	

14
DETACHED IMPULSIVE

People are magnetically drawn to these people as they appear exciting and yet aloof. A karmic vibration that is impulsive by nature. They often jump in before thinking, learning by experience.

Adah	Claud	Jacoba	Luce	Slade
Addala	Clay	Janet	Luz	Sonja
Adela	Con	Janos	Mai	Stable
Aldo	Daha	Jason	Mame	Stacy
Aleda	Dai	Jaye	Mead	Stean
Alyssa	Deda	Jim	Meda	Tait
Anya	Dee	Jonas	Mee	Tasman
Asella	Duana	Joy	Mia	Tita
Assunta	Dusan	June	Naste	Tomas
Astra	Elan	Ku	Neal	Tui
Aura	Elna	Lacy	Ned	Tye
Alyssa	Else	Lane	Nesta	Udall
Balbo	Eme	Lann	Nysa	Ulga
Bart	Emma	Lara	Ole	Ummu
Basia	Euan	Lars	Paul	Unna
Bebe	Fay	Lena	Sabra	Ursa
Bella	Fuad	Leo	Sacha	Usman
Caleb	Ida	Lex	Sage	Utah
Cane	Ilsa	Lisa	Scott	Walda
Cara	Isla	Loma	Selma	Zada
Cassel	Itta	Lon	Senta	Zea
Chu	Jaak	Lotta	Shasta	

15
PERCEPTIVE BEWITCHING

A magnetic person with a keen sense of knowingness or sixth sense. Ability to attract others without trying. Has many friends.

Abbot	Aram	Colba	Edna	Hoa
Adar	Aston	Dane	Elana	Ian
Aden	Atlanta	Dara	Embla	Ina
Agnas	Aulay	Dawn	Esme	Isaac
Aida	Axel	Dean	Ewe	Jago
Ailsa	Barba	Delta	Gay	Jascha
Alena	Baume	Demas	Hall	Jemma
Alex	Belda	Dena	Hana	Jocasta
Alisa	Blade	Desma	Hans	Joel
Alon	Blanca	Dobbs	Hao	Judy
Ansel	Cassem	Edan	Hawa	Juno

Jussi	Mabel	Nola	Salema	Tibb
Lach	Macy	Nyssa	Sally	Tolla
Lasar	Maia	Osnat	Santje	Wade
Layla	Mara	Palm	Santo	Wen
Leaf	Math	Paula	Scout	Wesla
Leesa	Mattea	Peta	Seamus	Yajna
Lissa	Melba	Platt	Shaw	Yutta
Lita	Mija	Rae	Silas	Zana
Liu	Nadda	Rama	Stella	
Lona	Neala	Ran	Sultan	
Lotus	Neda	Saddam	Taka	
Lyn	Netta	Sadoc	Tatia	

16
PERFECTIONIST RECLUSIVE

A loner type who appears odd or different. Very selective, as searching for perfection in self and others. Can be over-critical.

Adon	Cadel	Inas	Onatas	Sian
Alanna	Cadmus	Jack	Oola	Sloan
Alart	Cali	Jakab	Ora	Steel
Alben	Callan	Jalon	Orea	Talbot
Alexa	Carl	Jera	Otto	Talia
Amadea	Cassia	Jill	Pallas	Tansy
Amanda	Chad	Jocea	Palma	Tanya
Amara	Cid	Joha	Papa	Thea
Amon	Cosmas	Lalota	Pascal	Todd
Anne	Danae	Lang	Paz	Toya
Aralt	Danuta	Laotsu	Peata	Ugo
Aran	Deana	Lila	Raama	Uland
Baez	Della	Lim	Rana	Ulema
Baraba	Dru	Lucy	Rasma	Wanda
Basil	Edana	Luis	Raul	Yael
Becan	Elga	Meg	Resa	Yale
Bede	Elle	Mona	Rula	Yates
Bhama	Ewan	Nanda	Sabella	Yuan
Bliss	Fen	Nara	Salena	Zabad
Brad	Gael	Nell	Sebald	Zosa
Bram	Gale	Noam	Sedna	
Buena	Gamal	Olaf	Seth	
Burt	Huw	Oman	Shana	

17
ORGANISER CONFIDENT

A natural leader who can organise and motivate others. Learns quickly, taking action in a fearless manner.

Abadi	Burl	Hadassa	Mahla	Saxby
Abbey	Cahn	Hale	Maka	Senan
Abram	Callula	Hamal	Mandu	Shay
Afra	Callum	Hassan	Marc	Sheba
Agale	Carla	Haya	Marta	Snow
Agapa	Casey	Jabez	Maru	Stacia
Agato	Caton	Jalil	Mascot	Sturt
Akala	Chan	Janne	Maude	Tadia
Alcott	Clara	Jatila	Maui	Tain
Allen	Cleo	Jeames	Mila	Tamar
Alton	Cloe	Jehu	Moses	Tarsus
Alyx	Coel	Jenna	Mura	Tauno
Amahl	Cole	Jessi	Naaman	Thos
Ambar	Curt	Joash	Nanna	Tina
Amund	Dagda	Josha	Natale	Titus
Anais	Dallan	Judah	Nissa	Toby
Ananda	Dante	Julia	Nita	Tran
Ancel	Delma	Justen	Nona	Tuomas
Angus	Dura	Justis	Nui	Tuson
Annan	Dusty	Jytte	Nye	Tybalt
Anno	Dyan	Kae	Obed	Ure
Arana	Dyna	Kama	Olga	Ursus
Atho	Eben	Klaas	Opal	Wells
August	Eldad	Ko	Padma	Wyatt
Austen	Eli	Lance	Pia	Wyn
Baden	Eneas	Laura	Pola	Yen
Bapp	Enos	Leah	Ray	Yetta
Beth	Erl	Leota	Reta	Zanta
Betsy	Esara	Liam	Rosa	Zela
Bill	Fawn	Lida	Ross	Zela
Bina	Fleta	Lin	Rue	Zeus
Bnar	Gaby	Luisa	Ruma	Zulu
Boaz	Gleb	Lupus	Samara	
Brae	Gosta	Lyall	Samuel	
Bran	Guy	Magda	Sarama	

18
LEADER VOLUNTEER

This person wants to make the world a better place for all to live. Is able to relate to others with tolerance and love, using natural leadership abilities.

Abduh	Butch	Halse	Madde	Samuela
Acacia	Cadman	Helsa	Madoc	Sandy
Acima	Cain	Hew	Mahala	Selby
Adele	Carma	Hsuan	Marla	Shamus
Adila	Cera	Hunt	Maura	Shaun
Aeneas	Chase	Ilse	Mayo	Shem
Agia	Chuca	Imam	Mei	Shou
Ahmad	Cian	Jahdal	Melea	Sile
Alard	Coco	Jake	Mie	Soane
Alaura	Conal	Jansen	Moya	Stack
Alden	Cooba	Jareb	Mulga	Stuart
Aldis	Dacia	Jaret	Musetta	Suzan
Aldous	Dagan	Jayme	Myall	Syra
Alie	Dago	Jeff	Nadel	Tacita
Alston	Dalia	Jody	Nastaya	Talissa
Anita	Dalman	Jones	Natsha	Tamara
Ansell	Damsel	Kao	Nelda	Tammy
Anson	Darata	Kawa	Nial	Tania
Areta	Dei	Kum	Nila	Tenae
Asaph	Dibbs	Lagana	Nils	Thalassa
Aster	Duane	Lain	Odessa	Tully
Attila	Earl	Lamar	Oona	Tutapu
Augusta	Edsel	Lani	Otis	Udell
Austell	Egan	Latona	Paola	Walsh
Autumn	Elen	Lear	Patsy	Wang
Bambi	Elia	Lene	Patya	Welda
Belle	Elly	Leola	Pell	Yara
Beno	Elmo	Lina	Poma	Yasuf
Bert	Enz	Lotte	Red	Ynes
Betha	Eudo	Luella	Sabin	Ytha
Betty	Fazl	Luka	Saleh	Zales
Bijan	Fox	Lupe	Salid	Zetta
Billa	Gable	Lyle	Salim	Zia
Bret	Hai	Mabon	Samson	

19
AUTHORITY DOMINEERING

The person with this energy will meet with fateful opportunities as 19 is a karmic vibration. An authoritative figure who can be domineering. Must learn not to manipulate situations and/or people.

Adalia	Alain	Almena	Amida	Anica
Addis	Alameda	Aloha	Amie	Anselm
Afic	Albacett	Amadeus	Amin	Anton
Agnes	Alix	Amalia	Anaru	Aodh
Aime	Allyn	Amandus	Ancia	Aretas

Ari	Dix	Joey	Nadale	Shai
Ashby	Donal	Joli	Naldo	Shauna
Ashlea	Donata	Josef	Nance	Shen
Aurea	Douna	Kalla	Nastasya	Sissy
Azalea	Duff	Kate	Natasha	Sky
Babette	Eden	Kay	Natoma	Sri
Balunn	Edra	Klaus	Neco	Stacey
Bazel	Elena	Lacey	Neysa	Susie
Beli	Elias	Lalita	Noel	Sutton
Berta	Elisa	Latham	Oria	Suzy
Bice	Erma	Leena	Orm	Tallis
Blaze	Fabia	Leoda	Osanna	Tamati
Bobby	Fausto	Leon	Ostia	Tarn
Bono	Felda	Letha	Pablo	Tito
Boyd	Fudo	Liana	Pati	Trant
Brant	Fuji	Libusa	Patty	Treat
Bray	Gabela	Lilac	Peg	True
Bunty	Ganan	Lilla	Pejo	Tuck
Caddy	Gil	Liso	Pita	Tunde
Cadell	Gye	Lois	Plato	Tynam
Caera	Haleb	Lora	Poul	Tyne
Caley	Hapu	Lucia	Rafu	Ualtar
Cameo	Hara	Lynus	Rand	Urana
Cassius	Heo	Mabella	Ria	Waldo
Cesar	Hoda	Mack	Rod	Wally
Cilla	Holt	Madra	Rute	Ward
Claude	Hsia	Mahes	Ruy	Wei
Coen	Hudd	Maida	Sabina	Ysabel
Conn	Ilana	Malena	Sagar	Yules
Cora	Iola	Matiu	Saldia	Zane
Cushla	Ira	Matui	Salida	Zara
Cyr	Isi	Meade	Sancha	Zena
Dahna	Jayne	Midas	Sanson	Zoe
Dawed	Jewel	Mina	Saxon	
Dina	Joanna	Molan	Seton	

20
TECHNICAL COLLABORATOR

Someone who operates best behind the scenes and is often the power behind the throne. Has a technical mind that can overflow with details.

Adina	Aine	Anston	Arne	Balin
Adley	Alpha	Antons	Arod	Barbea
Adolf	Alter	Arafat	Athela	Bazza
Agatha	Althea	Arbel	Athol	Bento
Aidan	Ammon	Aria	Aubin	Blain

Blenda	Ermas	Jaime	Nain	Sosanna
Brett	Erna	Jair	Nani	Stefan
Bruna	Estella	Jamie	Narda	Sybyl
Buddy	Euclea	Jamin	Narn	Tallara
Burns	Eustace	Jared	Nemo	Tegan
Cadfan	Ewen	Jarett	Neola	Theda
Caesar	Fagan	John	Nina	Thom
Calista	Flann	Joletta	Noah	Tilo
Cary	Gage	Joshua	Nolan	Tobia
Cassie	Gail	Julius	Omar	Tomaso
Celesta	Galatea	Kadla	Onesta	Tony
Chou	Galem	Keal	Oonta	Tynan
Conan	Gamel	Koba	Oram	Udele
Cort	Gaye	Kuo	Oscar	Ueli
Cosmo	Glen	Lalage	Oswald	Ulalia
Cowan	Gold	Laurus	Page	Ulima
Cyra	Gupta	Leka	Pandu	Ulyana
Dacey	Gustaf	Leli	Paulo	Urban
Damon	Hajar	Leona	Pitt	Ursula
Danetta	Hallam	Liz	Rames	Uyeda
Dayle	Halle	Loch	Rena	Uzi
Deane	Hanna	Loyd	Rewa	Uzza
Debby	Hart	Lyman	Rex	Wajid
Debi	Hati	Lynda	Risa	Warda
Demos	Hatty	Lynn	Roma	Ware
Diana	Hebe	Lyra	Ron	Watson
Dora	Hella	Macey	Ruel	Weema
Dugan	Hui	Madon	Sadie	Wenda
Dural	Hume	Manly	Salmon	Wolf
Duscha	Hyam	Marama	Salome	Yolla
Dylan	Hyatt	Marea	Sancia	Yusuf
Edon	Igal	Meara	Sarah	Zak
Ehud	Ines	Menes	Scilla	Zella
Eliab	Ino	Menna	Seaton	Zenas
Elissa	Ion	Miao	Selena	Zita
Elita	Irja	Myles	Senalda	Zona
Elli	Isbel	Myuna	Shane	Zsa Zsa
Elwy	Isis	Na'amah	Sileas	
Emmett	Isola	Nadia	Sine	
Enola	Iwan	Naeem	Siusan	
Eran	Jaclyn	Naida	Sonya	

21
LOYAL SOCIAL
Extremely socially conscientious. Cultivates friends and is fiercely loyal.
Often the centre of attention. When upset, energies are easily scattered.

Adelle	Chen	Isabel	Maresa	Sandra
Adora	Clare	Jamina	Mary	Saturn
Adrana	Clio	Jarod	Meru	Shanna
Agape	Cluny	Jasmin	Milda	Shona
Aglia	Cocha	Jemmy	Mort	Sion
Agnessa	Colby	Jessica	Myee	Solon
Akuna	Cong	Jessop	Myra	Steele
Algar	Dalton	Jock	Nahum	Sunny
Alice	Damita	Johan	Nancy	Susanne
Allard	Dancel	Jolanda	Natham	Suzi
Allie	Deanna	Jonah	Natlia	Swain
Alwyn	Debra	Joram	Neoma	Tanton
Amber	Doane	Julie	Ngoc	Tatiana
Amnon	Donan	Justin	Niall	Teagan
Amyntas	Donna	Kai	Noble	Tepaea
Andras	Duncan	Kamala	Nolana	Thane
Angel	Dunstan	Kee	Nora	Theo
Annetta	Eamon	Ken	Nurla	Tien
Annis	Eber	Knut	Nyah	Tobias
Anwyl	Edson	Lako	Odell	Tolman
Argus	Edwy	Lamont	Oleg	Tullia
Arisa	Ekala	Lanny	Oran	Tyson
Arno	Ellen	Latif	Oro	Uffo
Aron	Ellis	Laure	Osmar	Ugon
Aspasia	Elton	Lawson	Oswalda	Ulani
Astarte	Embia	Lazlo	Owen	Uluka
Attracta	Emey	Leila	Pagan	Ulysses
Augustus	Emil	Leland	Pamela	Umei
Aurel	Erasma	Lelia	Pansy	Uri
Austin	Esdras	Lesbia	Pascha	Wallace
Aylee	Essie	Leura	Paton	Wanetta
Babilla	Esteban	Lide	Patti	Wayamba
Barr	Eswen	Lind	Pearce	Weiss
Basile	Ethan	Linus	Per	Welya
Beagan	Flanna	Lisle	Petula	Willa
Bern	Fleet	Liza	Phuc	Wisan
Bianca	Fulco	Llawela	Ranalt	Wystan
Bijou	Galen	Lowana	Rasia	Xina
Blaise	Gard	Luise	Reg	Yago
Bonosa	Gemma	Lyell	Rey	Yedda
Branca	Geza	Madge	Ric	Yin
Brand	Golda	Maelle	Rita	Zebada
Bree	Heult	Magnus	Rona	Zelda
Byng	Holla	Major	Rose	Zelma
Cacre	Hosea	Mandy	Ruby	
Calida	Husha	Manon	Ruza	
Camila	Ifan	Manuel	Sador	
Celia	Iona	Marcus	Salaome	

22
BUILDER BALANCE STRENGTH

A master vibration gives this person a strong desire to make or build, not only materially but ideally. Has determined strength to follow through with projects. Recognition is often given, due to their success.

Aaron	Cari	Ewart	Kyla	Penn
Abadie	Carlo	Eyar	Kym	Quoda
Abner	Carol	Faina	Lamballe	Rabia
Adler	Carr	Gaston	Lancia	Raissa
Ahmed	Casilda	Gene	Lawton	Raoul
Alaster	Caspar	Gera	Leni	Raye
Albert	Castor	Gill	Lily	Rayma
Albret	Celena	Gina	Linda	Remus
Alcina	Chara	Gian	Lira	Roy
Alder	Ciar	Glyn	Ljubica	Rufus
Allanah	Cien	Gwen	Logan	Rune
Alred	Clancy	Habib	Loila	Russel
Alysia	Cleon	Hagan	Lolly	Rusty
Alyssha	Clint	Halia	Louis	Ruth
Anastasia	Clyde	Hannu	Lubin	Ryan
Angela	Coletta	Hanya	Luke	Sachi
Annabel	Coral	Hayes	Lyncus	Saki
Ansley	Cullen	Hedda	Lynfa	Salih
Anthea	Daisy	Hoel	Lyulf	Sallie
Anwell	Danella	Huon	Mandel	Seanne
Arabela	Danil	Ideal	Manka	Selway
Arnall	Danny	Iduna	Manuela	Sewell
Ashur	Darel	Inga	Mayra	Sibly
Athena	Darya	Ismay	Megan	Sinbad
Audre	Delia	Jacinta	Melia	Solita
Auguste	Demi	Jacques	Mestra	Sonia
Austina	Denys	Jeanne	Milan	Speed
Bardo	Donalta	Jessie	Miles	Stanway
Barnabas	Donatus	Josie	Milo	Starr
Begga	Dugald	Jotham	Mladen	Stein
Benen	Duran	Joyce	Monte	Storm
Beulah	Dysis	Juanita	Mullaya	Suzsi
Bibi	Edwald	Julian	Murna	Sybil
Blake	Elmar	Julio	Nastassia	Taddeo
Blyth	Elston	Junius	Natalia	Taffy
Bobak	Emanuel	Kane	Nathan	Tamsin
Boden	Emelda	Kara	Neil	Tandia
Bozo	Emmett	Katya	Noleta	Taree
Bron	Erastus	Kean	Owena	Tarra
Bruce	Ernst	Kell	Paget	Teddy
Camden	Ester	Kit	Paloma	Thebe
Candace	Eudia	Kwan	Penda	Thomas

Toku	Ultima	Walton	Wray	Yera
Toni	Umina	Welby	Wullun	Yung
Tracy	Waite	Welsh	Wynn	Zaid
Udolf	Walcott	Wilda	Yani	Zalman
Ulisse	Wallis	Wilma	Yarn	Zaneta

23
ADVENTURER INNOVATIVE

A person with a sense of change and adventure. Sensitive to outer energies and able to see possibilities in situations.

Adalard	Bing	Darby	Garalt	Kaisa
Alair	Bjorn	Denby	Gesar	Kasia
Alastor	Blanka	Dewi	Gladys	Kayla
Alberta	Blossom	Dolly	Gould	Kent
Aldabella	Bonar	Domela	Gully	Knud
Alfonsa	Bonne	Donald	Hacon	Koo
Alisha	Bowen	Drew	Haldana	Ladislas
Allunga	Boyce	Duke	Hamar	Lanzo
Almond	Boyle	Dyfan	Hamlet	Laurana
Alwin	Brady	Eachan	Hansel	Laurans
Alyson	Brent	Earle	Hera	Leif
Amalie	Brita	Easter	Hina	Lemuel
Amelia	Brona	Ebert	Hsin	Lenis
Amico	Buri	Edie	Huey	Lewis
Amir	Burr	Edin	Hung	Libby
Amity	Byram	Egon	Iago	Lief
Ananias	Cadfael	Eldon	Iden	Lion
Anatole	Callista	Elene	Idetta	Lloyd
Arbell	Caren	Elian	Irma	Loni
Arlen	Carlos	Elise	Isaak	Lore
Arold	Carly	Ellyn	Ismael	Louisa
Artemas	Caryl	Elsie	Issur	Lucie
Ashlee	Caspara	Emer	Janelle	Luiz
Ashton	Catlin	Enid	Jarita	Lyndal
Auburn	Cecil	Eramus	Jayden	Lystra
Audley	Ceres	Esko	Jenks	Madlena
Aymon	Chantal	Estera	Jenny	Mahra
Azzo	Conlan	Ethel	Jerald	Mair
Balbina	Custance	Ettie	Joanne	Malchus
Baron	Cyrus	Eustella	Joelle	Malise
Belica	Dagon	Ezra	Jorg	Mamie
Berg	Damalis	Fadil	Jory	Mancia
Bessie	Danica	Fatima	Josif	Marah
Bethan	Danila	Fayme	Juliana	Marco
Bika	Dannel	Filma	Juliet	Mari

Marsh	Paddy	Sabine	Swetlana	Wayne
Media	Paley	Samantha	Teague	Whetu
Mere	Panacea	Sarita	Tempe	Wistan
Mira	Pania	Sarka	Teresa	Xenos
Molly	Paolo	Sarona	Thelma	Yancy
Nannos	Pascoe	Sayer	Thomasa	Yarna
Nelia	Patton	Semele	Ting	Yilla
Nico	Piet	Serle	Tommy	Yrjo
Nidda	Radha	Shallum	Tonia	Zack
Niels	Ramsay	Shalom	Trella	Zdena
Niles	Randal	Shima	Trent	Zenda
Ninus	Reed	Signa	Tuesday	Zera
Oake	Renata	Sixte	Turi	Zina
Omega	Rhea	Soter	Tyre	Zusane
Osmanna	Rima	Spain	Upton	
Osmund	Roald	St John	Urbi	
Ouida	Rudy	Suria	Walden	

24
PARENTAL GIVER

A real people person. Compelled to assist and give to others. Must take care not to become used. Must learn to be assertive.

Adabelle	Ballina	Cadwell	Denis	Elora
Adair	Baptist	Cahil	Denman	Emera
Adria	Barak	Calantha	Diane	Emina
Agathe	Barbra	Camilla	Dilys	Emlyn
Agilus	Barnet	Carisa	Dinna	Emmon
Aiden	Barnum	Cawley	Dino	Epona
Aimee	Bayard	Celeste	Dion	Erasmus
Alaine	Beathan	Chang	Dobson	Ermo
Allambee	Benita	Claudia	Donalda	Estelle
Ambler	Benson	Cosette	Donato	Ezzat
Andie	Bhima	Cosima	Dorcas	Fabian
Andre	Billy	Culley	Dore	Fabio
Aniela	Bird	Cuong	Dougal	Falcon
Annali	Blair	Cybil	Druce	Fanny
Annica	Bodil	Dagny	Duarte	Fossetta
Anyon	Booth	Dalenna	Durant	Franc
Arden	Borg	Damian	Dustin	Frants
Arend	Britt	Damosel	Eberta	Fred
Armand	Bryan	Danette	Edina	Frost
Artur	Bryna	Darcy	Eglah	Gabin
Asher	Burne	Daria	Eira	Galton
Ava	Butler	Daryl	Elaeth	Gary
Balder	Byblis	Delano	Ellamay	Gilad

Gilda	Jitka	Lorna	Orela	Sorel
Grant	Jobina	Louella	Paora	Stanley
Gray	Jolie	Loyce	Paschal	Stark
Greta	Justice	Lucina	Peach	Sulwyn
Guida	Kacha	Ludlow	Pepe	Suzanna
Gwyn	Kahla	Lycon	Petar	Tabari
Haley	Kalah	Lydia	Petra	Tahlia
Halona	Kali	Madalena	Prue	Tallulah
Hamon	Kang	Mahmud	Rahul	Taralga
Hatton	Karl	Mahon	Rani	Tarati
Heath	Kassia	Malcolm	Remo	Tekea
Hedy	Katia	Malone	Rene	Tetley
Helga	Katra	Manchu	Rilta	Thalia
Herb	Kawana	Manoel	Rina	Thanh
Hetty	Kaye	Marcos	Rio	Tilly
Hone	Kelda	Maree	Rise	Tobie
Howe	Kemel	Maria	Rolf	Topaz
Huang	Kim	Maris	Rolo	Tory
Hugo	Kosmas	Marsha	Rosel	Trista
Hurd	Kura	Mataora	Roseta	Troy
Hyde	Kyna	Matilda	Rosh	Truly
Iain	Lachlan	Maxim	Roza	Truman
Ileana	Lamech	Melissa	Ruben	Tudor
Ilka	Landon	Melita	Saladin	Tulip
Ilona	Lark	Menia	Sancho	Ulmer
Inia	Laurel	Minna	Sarid	Uric
Iolo	Leanne	Moshe	Scarlet	Ursell
Ithaca	Learna	Nambur	Searle	Urson
Jacinda	Leewan	Natuska	Sebert	Uxor
Jakk	Lelica	Nitya	Seldon	Wen De
Janice	Lemuela	Noelda	Selina	Weston
Japhet	Lennan	Obert	Serah	Wren
Jasper	Lesley	Odette	Shani	Yasser
Jemima	Lilah	Olwen	Sibella	Zeno
Jennel	Lili	Omer	Siloam	Zilla
Jered	Linet	Onyx	Skye	Zora
Jeri	Lolita	Orbana	Smith	

25
ANALYTICAL SCIENTIFIC

Seekers of knowledge who analyse everything. Have gifted minds that often makes them a perfect scientist or investigative researcher.

Abdullah	Agatho	Alethea	Alison	Amaris
Adamina	Ainslea	Alexis	Amador	Anders
Adoni	Akim	Alger	Amalthea	Andrea

Andres	Celie	Faisel	Jaimee	Micah
Annette	Cerys	Farr	Jannali	Mimosa
Annie	Chaim	Fern	Jarman	Minet
Aquila	Chanel	Finn	Jemina	Ming
Arabella	Cher	Fitz	Jenni	Minos
Armon	Chin	Flint	Jerom	Mitra
Ashley	Chloe	Flora	Jilli	Moise
Auryn	Clair	Fonz	Jimmy	Morna
Ayfara	Claresta	Ford	Jodie	Muir
Aylie	Codey	Freda	Jorah	Mungo
Azora	Colgan	Fulton	Kadi	Naarah
Baird	Comyn	Gabor	Kanya	Nanette
Banquo	Constant	Galahad	Karla	Naomi
Baptista	Cory	Gatian	Klara	Neddy
Barbara	Crocus	Gazza	Kunama	Nelson
Barica	Curra	Gildas	Kurt	Nero
Barton	Cutler	Giles	Labhras	Ngaru
Baxter	Cybele	Gitana	Lachman	Nguen
Beldon	Dalasaid	Glenda	Laing	Nino
Belina	Damiana	Glenn	Lanelle	Noni
Bellamy	Damzel	Grace	Larissa	Norma
Benton	Daron	Gytha	Larson	Odolf
Bercan	Deanne	Haig	Lascelles	Oeneus
Bered	Denisa	Halim	Lauri	Oren
Bernal	Desley	Halstead	Leewana	Osbert
Bethel	Dianna	Halton	Leko	Paques
Bjorg	Dibble	Hank	Lenka	Payne
Blaine	Donia	Hanno	Lester	Pearl
Blaxland	Doran	Hashum	Lewanna	Pleasant
Bonamy	Douglas	Haydn	Lilly	Quamby
Bonita	Doyle	Hazel	Lindal	Rafael
Bonny	Ebony	Helmut	Lowell	Raina
Boswell	Edmund	Heng	Lucelle	Ramon
Brie	Efram	Heutte	Luciana	Ranee
Bruno	Elgar	Hilda	Ludolf	Remy
Burk	Eliot	Hilma	Lynne	Reseda
Cadiz	Ellie	Hsuang	Lytton	Rheta
Calder	Ellin	Hue Lan	Maddox	Rhun
Calisto	Eloisa	Hyman	Magali	Rhys
Calleen	Elwyn	Icabod	Mallard	Ricca
Carey	Elyne	Idona	Manley	Rilla
Carissa	Emry	Inara	Manoah	Rimu
Carita	Engel	Inari	Marcel	Rip
Carlota	Ennis	Innes	Mark	Rois
Carmel	Ertha	Ione	Martha	Roman
Carson	Esmond	Isabella	Matong	Ronda
Casandra	Eulalia	Ismena	Maxima	Russell
Catalina	Eustacia	Jacqui	Melany	Sadira

Sampson	Sheena	Tabitha	Tuki	Wolfe
Sander	Shenae	Tearle	Ungar	Wystand
Saraid	Sibila	Tegyd	Waine	Yaralla
Schuman	Simon	Terza	Walter	Ynez
Seabert	Sinead	Thera	Waris	Zesk
Sefton	Solina	Thor	Warra	Zoltan
Seward	Stewart	Trawalla	Wilga	
Shaina	Susannah	Trudy	Wille	

26
PROSPEROUS GENEROUS

A person who is motivated to be successful. Has a loving and generous nature. Can be extravagant, often spending more than they have.

Abdarah	Baruch	Corel	Eydis	Hazael
Abraham	Basilia	Cormac	Faine	Helen
Adonia	Beattie	Crystal	Faith	Hemi
Adonis	Bendis	Cynara	Farand	Hong
Alaric	Bennett	Dagmar	Fastmund	Hope
Albion	Beryl	Dahlia	Finan	Horst
Aldred	Bettina	Daphna	Finna	Hugh
Alester	Biddy	Debor	Flannan	Icarus
Alicia	Bobbie	Delmar	Fleur	Imelda
Alisson	Bondi	Deodatus	Floyd	Inge
Allyson	Bowral	Desmona	Flynn	Ireta
Alroy	Braden	Dewey	Gair	Isobel
Amery	Bradman	Donnan	Galina	Janine
Anarawd	Brenda	Dory	Gaspar	Jareth
Anastasie	Brian	Douglass	Gelon	Jasmine
Anastatius	Bryce	Dudley	Gerda	Jeanette
Andreas	Burnum	Durand	Gisela	Jerara
Angele	Caddie	Dynawd	Glenna	Johann
Annabella	Cadence	Eartha	Gorm	Joktan
Anstice	Callagun	Edgar	Guild	Jordan
Antony	Camelia	Eduard	Hagar	Joris
Apollo	Carmela	Elder	Hagen	Josiah
Aretha	Cassandra	Eliza	Halden	Julien
Ariana	Cassidy	Elmer	Haldis	Justine
Arora	Celene	Elysia	Halima	Kamballa
Astrid	Ceri	Emile	Halmar	Kani
Ayleen	Chelsea	Emrys	Hamid	Kelso
Aylwen	Chera	Ensor	Handel	Kenn
Barclay	Colette	Eric	Hapai	Kera
Barden	Colin	Ernacta	Harald	Kina
Barlow	Combara	Eryn	Hastin	Kunaama
Barnett	Concha	Ethell	Hayne	Kung

Kupe	Minh	Pileb	Shanti	Trung
Kyle	Minya	Polly	Shelah	Tullio
Laird	Mischa	Pomme	Shelby	Tyler
Lambert	Moesen	Powys	Shih	Ulfer
Lauren	Mosera	Quebec	Sholto	Unity
Lauretta	Mosina	Radella	Sienna	Uyeno
Lauris	Myrna	Rahel	Simona	Val
Lawler	Naarai	Ramona	Sophus	Walwyn
Lazard	Naashom	Randall	Sperata	Wark
Lazarus	Nadelle	Randy	Starlee	Wayland
Lazzo	Nancye	Rhett	Stefano	Weber
Leslie	Natalie	Rice	Straton	Welton
Lowanna	Nessie	Roch	Sulien	Wen Hu
Madonna	Newell	Romana	Summer	Wendy
Mahura	Nguon	Romula	Suzette	Wesley
Manasseh	Nicol	Ronan	Sylwen	Woltsha
Marita	Nili	Ropata	Tacitah	Wulfstan
Marli	Norna	Rosetta	Tahnia	Xanthus
Maroo	Nydia	Rosia	Talitha	Xenia
Marten	Obelia	Rowan	Taranga	Xylia
Massimo	Olney	Saisho	Tarni	Yatmund
Mathena	Olono	Salomon	Tempest	Yelena
Mathias	Onslow	Samaria	Theon	Yeshe
Mayer	Orell	Sanders	Thiess	Yury
Melina	Orsola	Scarlett	Thora	Zako
Mellisa	Osmond	Scobie	Tibelda	Zelia
Mendel	Oswin	Seaward	Timon	Zelman
Merle	Pachet	Selwyn	Toplas	
Messina	Parlan	Serena	Tori	
Milly	Parr	Shanais	Tottie	
Mimi	Pelias	Shandy	Trina	

27
PEACEFUL DEVOTED

A pacifist by nature, this person sees the beauty and potential in all. Often drawn to people in need of help and encouragement.

Abrabella	Anika	Audree	Billee	Breese
Achill	Annora	Audwin	Blanche	Brenna
Ailie	Antonya	Ayward	Blythe	Briana
Aladdin	Araluen	Azelia	Bogart	Bryde
Alastair	Ariel	Aziza	Boolee	Burton
Aldwin	Artina	Bailey	Booral	Cadenza
Alva	Ascelin	Barnaby	Boris	Cahill
Amory	Ashlin	Beppo	Bowie	Cailean
Angelo	Aubrey	Bertha	Brandan	Calandra

Caldwell	Elijah	Holmes	Margo	Renaud
Camira	Eliott	Homi	Marius	Renay
Carin	Elisha	Hosanna	Marlee	Rexana
Carlotta	Elmina	Howel	Marlen	Rhyl
Carmen	Elwin	Hudson	Maryse	Roanna
Carole	Emanuela	Idabell	Matthew	Rocco
Chantel	Emelia	Idalia	Maxwell	Rollo
Charo	Enoch	Idette	Meegan	Rosabel
Chilla	Erica	Illeana	Mick	Rosane
Chueh	Erland	Imre	Modeste	Rumon
Clark	Ernald	Ithel	Moffatt	Salaidh
Clayton	Ernest	Izod	Morag	Sebastian
Clement	Euclid	Johanna	Munro	Serge
Cliff	Faustin	Jordana	Nadege	Sheila
Clydai	Felton	Josaphat	Nafanael	Shelly
Clydia	Fidel	Judith	Nartee	Signe
Cohen	Fiona	Justino	Nerys	Sorell
Coleman	Fletch	Kaare	Nicola	Spira
Colina	Fu Hai	Kacey	Noelle	Stanislaus
Colley	Gaetano	Kathe	Noora	Sterne
Concetta	Gamlyn	Keane	Nowell	Sumner
Consuela	Garman	Kemp	Odile	Syria
Conway	Garth	Kimba	Ogden	Talebin
Curtis	Gelasia	Kolet	Onora	Tecwyn
Cybill	Gerada	Kora	Orella	Terese
Dagmara	Gero	Kuang	Orissa	Thank
Daniel	Gino	Kurd	Orsch	Theano
Dargan	Githa	Kuyan	Orson	Thetis
Darius	Glynn	Laxzlo	Oxley	Thibaut
Darton	Gore	Lazare	Padarn	Thyra
Daryll	Gwenda	Leith	Paine	Tiaio
Debbie	Hadden	Lenard	Pamina	Tracey
Delwen	Haldane	Lilli	Pancras	Troth
Denham	Halina	Lior	Paree	Uberto
Dick	Halley	Lisette	Paris	Ulger
Dinah	Hari	Lori	Paxton	Ulric
Donella	Harlan	Lottie	Penia	Undina
Dragan	Hattie	Louise	Pero	Urian
Dulcie	Haynes	Luthais	Petica	Ursin
Dwayne	Heaton	Maarten	Phebe	Vaal
Eadgar	Hein	Madri	Placid	Vala
Edbert	Helena	Mahalia	Quenes	Waratah
Eddie	Heni	Mahlon	Ralston	Warka
Egor	Hiew	Maicaela	Ramsey	Wen Li
Eilis	Hinda	Malinda	Reece	Wenona
Elberta	Hine	Marcia	Regan	Willy
Eleni	Holly	Mardi	Reid	Wynne
Elfleda	Holman	Marelda	Remi	Xanthe

| Xylon | Yasmin | Yolanda | Zahra | Zubin |
| Yarra | Yigal | Yoram | Zared | |

28
LEADER ORGANISER

A born leader with great organising abilities. Abundantly self-confident; must guard against exaggeration and extravagance.

Abigael	Bepin	Cristal	Gawain	Jolyon
Achilla	Berge	Crosby	Gazella	Jorge
Adelina	Bethesda	Cyndi	Gearalt	Joseph
Ahern	Bilyana	Damien	Gelges	Jubilee
Ahren	Boguslaw	Daniela	Gemmel	Kalid
Aidhan	Branch	Defail	Gilah	Kalila
Aigneis	Brandy	Delora	Gilboa	Kalyan
Aileen	Brice	Drina	Gittle	Kamil
Alberto	Brites	Drostan	Giulo	Katie
Alfonso	Brody	Druella	Giusto	Kaylea
Alfred	Bruin	Earnest	Glenys	Kelby
Allison	Brynn	Edith	Goetz	Kiel
Alpheus	Burden	Edmond	Grady	Knox
Ambrose	Burgess	Edris	Greg	Kolya
Amelina	Burnett	Edward	Grete	Kono
Amparo	Byrne	Edwin	Guisto	Kort
Antaine	Cabarita	Elaine	Haddon	Krys
Antoni	Calypso	Eldora	Hadley	Kuei
Aristo	Camille	Electra	Haido	Kyne
Arlene	Campbell	Elihu	Hannah	Lancelot
Arnold	Carina	Ellice	Hearn	Landers
Asteria	Cecile	Elliot	Hellmut	Laurent
Aurnia	Celosia	Emily	Hero	Lawren
Austonia	Cheng	Erin	Hobart	Layaleeta
Bahadur	Cindy	Ernesta	Honesta	Lindall
Baker	Cissie	Essylit	Hozo	Lindy
Baldred	Clarissa	Eudora	Hussain	Linnea
Balthasar	Clarita	Eva	Hywel	Llewella
Bambalina	Claudette	Fabien	Ilone	Lonie
Barbie	Cleantha	Fagin	Indra	Loren
Barret	Cleary	Fenella	Iris	Loretta
Barry	Clematis	Fidela	Isleen	Lorne
Bartram	Clythe	Flinn	Isolde	Lucien
Barwon	Conrad	Freya	Isreal	Lucinda
Beaumont	Consolata	Fulke	Ittamar	Lycidas
Becky	Content	Fushen	Jackson	Lynton
Benite	Coretta	Garbett	Jerusha	Madira
Benzel	Corra	Gasparas	Jiri	Mahuru

Maire	Nestor	Pelham	Serica	Uziel
Malchi	Nettie	Pelton	Shari	Van
Mander	Neumann	Peter	Sisile	Walmond
Mardia	Newton	Pramana	Skip	Wambalano
Marei	Ngaio	Probus	Socrates	Weldon
Marette	Nicolas	Quieta	Solange	Wendela
Mariam	Nidra	Quinta	Sorcha	Woody
Marie	Niku	Ralph	Spero	Xylona
Marlon	Nohah	Rebecca	St Clair	Yeoman
Marlow	Nyora	Renato	Suzanne	Ynyr
Matthias	Odelia	Renault	Tapanui	Young
Medina	Oldina	Rere	Tautiti	Yudesh
Mei Yu	Olien	Rhoda	Taylor	Yuri
Melania	Olinda	Rogan	Thaddeus	Zaira
Mercy	Orland	Roland	Tinka	Zandra
Meryl	Orton	Ronald	Traudi	Zanette
Michal	Oskar	Rosanna	Tshinta	Zaria
Milcah	Osric	Rosita	Udolfo	Zeeman
Milka	Otylia	Roxana	Uilleam	Zenia
Millett	Padgett	Sabrina	Ulicia	Zero
Milli	Paulette	Sandler	Ulrica	
Monica	Paulin	Saturday	Urania	
Nereus	Payton	Sawyer	Urszula	

29
WAY-SHOWER HUMANITARIAN
A master energy that makes this person a natural teacher. Has the ability and desire to direct ideas and philosophies to help others.

Aldelpha	Arabelle	Bedelia	Burgh	Claudina
Adolph	Ardley	Belinda	Burley	Claudio
Adrian	Ardolph	Benilda	Burnetta	Clytie
Ahearn	Arien	Benito	Byron	Collin
Aideen	Arnaldo	Benoit	Cadbury	Conor
Ainslee	Ashburn	Bentley	Calhoun	Coriss
Alfreda	Audrey	Bernabe	Camellia	Cosimo
Allegra	Audric	Bethlem	Camillo	Craig
Alleyne	Audrye	Bibiana	Capri	Crandall
Alonzo	Aurora	Biloela	Caragh	Cyria
Andree	Avan	Bligh	Caralyn	Cyryl
Andrew	Aylmer	Booran	Carilla	Damaris
Andria	Azaria	Boyden	Carlton	Darran
Antonetta	Baldwin	Bride	Carter	Dauntie
Antonia	Barney	Bronte	Cartin	Delice
Anzley	Bartley	Brunetta	Chapman	Delko
April	Basillia	Burdon	Chico	Delwyn

Delyth	Godart	Lucille	Orlanda	Tarrant
Denise	Guido	Luzian	Ormar	Teangi
Dennis	Gypsy	Lynette	Ormsby	Tegwen
Desmond	Gywnn	Lyonel	Osborn	Teobaldo
Dianne	Haines	Lyris	Paige	Tepene
Digby	Hallie	Maitland	Palmer	Themis
Dione	Hanley	Malachi	Panthea	Thibaud
Docilla	Hardy	Manolis	Pasquale	Thien
Domina	Haylee	Marcella	Paulina	Titania
Doree	Heber	Margot	Pendle	Topaze
Doretta	Hika	Marian	Penny	Trish
Doria	Hoyle	Marina	Phanessa	Tristan
Doris	Huatare	Mario	Phelan	Ulick
Drystan	Hubert	Marise	Pilar	Ulva
Edelyn	Imber	Marley	Pomona	Umeko
Edmonda	Innis	Marsden	Powell	Uriel
Edryd	Irena	McCadie	Rachel	Urmila
Edwina	Isabelle	Medora	Radley	Wakil
Egmont	Isaiah	Melantha	Raine	Waminda
Einar	Ismene	Melody	Raquel	Webster
Elgin	Jacinth	Melrosa	Rechaba	White
Eloise	Jarrah	Mike	Reina	Willem
Elwood	Jarred	Millar	Renee	Willi
Emelye	Jereme	Milton	Reuben	Wilmot
Endor	Jindra	Mintha	Rhona	Wilson
Endres	Jonathan	Modesty	Ritza	Winola
Erina	Jurgi	Modwen	Robyn	Witton
Estrella	Kambara	Moira	Rock	Wylie
Ettore	Karel	Monette	Roden	Wyralla
Euchar	Kathy	Moree	Rohan	Ximen
Eusebius	Katina	Moria	Rolanda	Yazid
Fabron	Kegan	Moulton	Romee	Yestin
Farid	Kelly	Muhammad	Romola	Zamora
Farold	Kendal	Nadine	Rufena	Zeke
Felix	Keyna	Nairn	Ryland	Zenanda
Fenton	Kobai	Narayan	Sanborn	Zika
Forbes	Kudno	Neryl	Sargon	Zonar
Forest	Kulka	Ngahue	Semira	Zoran
Franz	Larelle	Ngoc Nu	Septima	Zosima
Freyja	Larry	Nigel	Shaine	Zotica
Gannon	Leger	Nolene	Sharen	
Garnet	Lennon	Norah	Signy	
Garsias	Lettice	Nunciata	Steffi	
Gerald	Lilie	Odwin	Stephan	
Gerel	Linnet	Olympas	Sumika	
Gilead	Lister	Oralia	Sydney	
Gisella	Lombard	Orestes	Taggart	
Glenyss	Lorena	Orin	Tancred	

30
DRAMATIC JOYOUS

An entertainer who thrives on an audience. Often a drama queen. Has a natural ability to spread joy. Can appear flighty, scatterbrained.

Addison	Candice	Esther	Javan	Marshall
Adoree	Carice	Eugene	Jehudi	Martin
Adriana	Carlin	Eunice	Jerome	Masorah
Agathon	Carmenta	Fazio	Jerzy	Maxine
Akyssha	Carney	Fedor	Jocelyn	Maybelle
Alejandra	Cecily	Fenlon	Joselin	Mayhew
Alister	Celine	Fergu	Jurgen	Mayrah
Aloisia	Charles	Fifi	Kaarle	Meghan
Amarina	Chris	Filep	Kalina	Melony
Amethyst	Cicely	Finetta	Kari	Meyer
Ancika	Cindi	Finola	Karlo	Minella
Aneira	Claire	Frances	Karol	Minka
Angwyn	Colleen	Franco	Kaspar	Moibeal
Annabelle	Corey	Fulbert	Kathel	Muire
Ardelle	Corissa	Garcia	Kattie	Muzio
Ariane	Corona	Gaspard	Keaton	Myrtle
Arisai	Curran	Geoff	Kedar	Nellie
Armando	Cynfael	Gibson	Keelan	Nelwyn
Arturo	Cyrena	Gomez	Kern	Newbold
Arundel	Daphne	Graham	Kimbal	Nghia
Azarias	Darnell	Gualter	Kira	Ngoc Lan
Balfour	Delbert	Gunnar	Kris	Nike
Baptisto	Dermot	Hachman	Kurao	Niklas
Bardin	Diantha	Hadiya	Lainey	Nilton
Barrett	Dietman	Hafwen	Laurie	Ninon
Bathsheba	Dillon	Hamlin	Leiland	Noris
Beniah	Doron	Hayden	Lennox	Norman
Beppi	Drake	Hazim	Leroy	Ofrah
Berend	Eachunn	Hester	Leteesha	Omero
Bethany	Edison	Hollis	Lilian	Oneida
Beynon	Edric	Horeb	Lindsay	Orian
Birra	Egbert	Howell	Linton	Osgood
Brandi	Egide	Hsing	Liong	Otilia
Brecon	Eiros	Huberta	Lisbeth	Ozora
Briar	Elanora	Ianthe	Luciano	Parnel
Brien	Eldred	Isador	Luther	Peaches
Bronya	Elidr	Ithnan	Lyndon	Peder
Buadhach	Elliott	Izaak	Madison	Peony
Burke	Elrica	Jacintha	Magdalen	Perde
Burnell	Elroy	Jackie	Malory	Petros
Caesaria	Emery	Jagger	Marek	Phelp
Caitlyn	Emmanuel	Jarrod	Mariana	Phung

Pier	Rouge	Strachan	Turuwun	Ximena
Prima	Royce	Sveja	Ulfred	Yoko
Quenby	Sappho	Tahira	Uriah	Yootha
Quinn	Sargent	Temira	Uzair	Yugany
Rachael	Scholem	Tereza	Vlad	Zadok
Rasmussen	Serene	Thaine	Vlasta	Zahid
Rianna	Shanahan	Thirsa	Wandjuk	Zelotes
Richa	Sharon	Thistle	Wardell	Zilia
Riona	Sierna	Thorn	Wendell	Zofia
Rohana	Sigwald	Tizane	Willis	Zozel
Romuald	Simeon	Toireasa	Wilton	Zublin
Rosalia	Simone	Tremble	Wladyslaw	Zwetlana
Roscoe	Sirena	Trisha	Wybert	

31
ENDURING RITUALISTIC

This person has great patience and perseverance; can keep at things longer than most. Drawn to anything ritualistic. Has a good memory for special occasions.

Adelbert	Billie	Darice	Farley	Harold
Aderyn	Borden	Delinda	Fedora	Haydon
Adriel	Bradley	Denice	Felice	Hayley
Agipatus	Brendan	Dexter	Fergus	Helene
Ainsley	Brock	Diego	Fingal	Hiram
Akashi	Brunella	Diocles	Finlay	Hodaka
Akira	Carleen	Donegal	Fraser	Holden
Aloysius	Carlina	Dorak	Fursey	Honey
Antonella	Carlyle	Dorita	Galiena	Houston
Arialh	Catarina	Eckart	Garcias	Igor
Ariella	Cecilya	Effie	Garnett	Illeane
Arika	Cesilia	Eldwin	German	Illiana
Astride	Chandra	Elined	Gomer	Ingar
Auberon	Charis	Elisabetta	Gondol	Isadora
Audrie	Chiara	Elmira	Gough	Isambard
Aurelia	Chitty	Elspeth	Graeme	Ishmael
Aurella	Cloris	Elswyth	Grande	Jeremy
Auriol	Columbia	Elva	Gretel	Jermyn
Avel	Constance	Emerald	Gudrun	Jerry
Azaliah	Cranog	Emilia	Gwern	Jethro
Bardolf	Cristy	Emmanuela	Hagley	Jokim
Barnard	Cyrano	Emory	Hakon	Joscelyn
Barris	Cyril	Ercole	Hamish	Kaine
Benedetta	Daltrey	Eucaria	Hariata	Kanku
Bernia	Daniella	Eudocia	Harim	Karen
Berthe	Darcie	Failka	Harland	Karly

Kaylah	Magdalena	Nixon	Robin	Theone
Keely	Maloney	Nyomi	Roche	Theora
Ketura	Malva	Nyree	Roesia	Theresa
Kiara	Margaux	Obadiah	Romano	Tiki
Kitty	Margen	Oprah	Rory	Umberto
Kodai	Mariel	Oriana	Rosina	Undine
Kotka	Marko	Orpah	Roslyn	Urien
Krysta	Marney	Pedro	Rowena	Urith
Kuracca	Martina	Pepita	Ruzena	Usenko
Kyrus	Maynard	Percy	Saturnia	Valda
Langdon	Melinda	Perth	Seonaid	Vale
Langley	Mercia	Phelps	Sereno	Valma
Launcelot	Merton	Piers	Shahid	Vesta
Laureen	Miguel	Pilita	Shannon	Waminoa
Laurene	Mihai	Pippa	Sheelah	Welcome
Leontia	Millissa	Piran	Shoshana	Wensley
Letitia	Mishael	Pleasance	Sidney	Willow
Leupold	Mwynen	Psyche	Solomon	Wilmar
Linden	Myron	Qadir	Sulgwyn	Winona
Linette	Nardoo	Quabiz	Tahiti	Yolande
Lionel	Narelle	Quelita	Tarcoola	Yseulete
Ludger	Narrawa	Quintus	Tekura	Yung Fu
Ludwig	Nathanael	Ranelle	Templar	Zamir
Luigi	Naylor	Rangi	Tepko	
Lynelle	Nerissa	Regis	Terauara	
Lysandra	Nicolaus	Renita	Theobald	
Macarius	Nicole	Renny	Theola	

32
VERSATILE INQUISITIVE

This person will have a strong need for freedom, seeming restless. Able to do several things at once. A good storyteller.

Abigail	Annika	Bertram	Carine	Cliantha
Achille	Antinous	Bluesky	Carryl	Clymene
Adelaide	Antonica	Bonnie	Cathleen	Coniah
Adelberta	Argyle	Boreen	Catrice	Consuelo
Adelinda	Armide	Bradwell	Cavan	Corliss
Adeline	Arthur	Bramwell	Cerian	Cyngen
Agostina	Athanasius	Brandon	Cerise	Daniele
Aikane	Barron	Branwen	Chalice	Darerca
Almadine	Bellinda	Brazil	Cinnia	Darleen
Amarantha	Benhur	Brianna	Clarisse	Darlene
Amelinda	Benjamin	Brunton	Clarke	Dermott
America	Benoni	Callaghan	Cledwyn	Deva
Amorita	Berry	Candido	Clemente	Dinsdale

Donahue	Hafiz	Kendall	Odilia	Sidony
Eduardo	Haidee	Kerttu	Olav	Siobhan
Ehren	Hammond	Khaled	Olier	Sizie
Eileen	Harden	King	Olympe	Sophia
Eilene	Harlow	Klaudia	Opalina	Spiro
Eilwen	Haroun	Krita	Orfeo	Starbuck
Eleazar	Hava	Larine	Oriel	Sweetie
Elfred	Hedley	Leander	Ottilia	Tagwyn
Ellery	Heine	Leigh	Paschasia	Tearoha
Ellison	Herman	Leticia	Penina	Temmatenga
Elodie	Hermes	Lindon	Persia	Tenille
Elouera	Herod	Linley	Petunia	Teodor
Emmylou	Homer	Lorin	Phanuel	Terry
Erlina	Horace	Ludwiga	Phoebus	Trilby
Ermin	Hori	Macnair	Picton	Trudie
Erneste	Hoshi	Marcellus	Piltti	Uilliam
Ernold	Hughes	Markos	Pomare	Vassy
Errol	Hunter	Marlene	Quillan	Veda
Eryk	Hussein	Mathilda	Ragnar	Wagner
Eskaer	Huxley	Maureen	Ramiah	Wakely
Eurwen	Idealia	Mave	Rashid	Waldemar
Eve	Idris	Medwin	Raydon	Warrun
Farnell	Ilaria	Melanie	Rhain	Waterman
Farry	Inir	Melmoth	Rhina	Wenceslaus
Finbar	Iva	Meshullam	Rick	Willmot
Fiske	Izabella	Michel	Rigg	Xanthia
Frank	Jamieson	Miguela	Rinah	Xerxes
Galilah	Jerko	Minette	Robina	Yarran
Gandolf	Jimmie	Mitzi	Rodway	Yartuwe
Gareth	Joachim	Modred	Rosalyn	Yasmine
Garmon	Johannes	Morgan	Rosanne	Zaidee
Gemalli	Johanon	Morton	Roscius	Zamira
Ghafar	Johnson	Nathania	Rosslyn	Zander
Giotto	Kabir	Newlin	Ruik	Zebulon
Gladney	Katalin	Nguyen	Sanford	Zelig
Gladwyn	Katri	Nirah	Sebastiane	Zillah
Glynis	Keefe	Nouri	Septimus	Zohar
Gwandalan	Keenan	Nymbin	Serilda	
Haakon	Kelham	Nympha	Sheldon	
Hackett	Kelsey	Odelette	Shelley	

33
TEACHER COUNSELLOR

A master energy that will have the opportunity to reach many. Creative in their approach. Teaching and counselling come naturally, but they must learn to detach.

Achilles	Dagwood	Hakim	Maryjane	Renaldo
Adaminah	Dalziel	Halcyon	Marylou	Renard
Adrien	Darien	Harley	Maurilla	Rheese
Adrine	Darren	Harmon	Melrose	Rhonda
Ainslie	Darryl	Hector	Merlyn	Riley
Amfrid	Darwin	Helice	Michael	Robert
Andrei	Delfina	Henare	Michi	Roeland
Antoine	Delilah	Hertha	Millard	Rongo
Arva	Delores	Hilton	Miller	Rosamund
Augustinas	Derain	Howard	Mirabel	Rowland
Aurore	Derina	Ichabod	Miranda	Ruark
Avoca	Derwen	Irene	Montague	Rupulle
Belva	Dhatri	Irina	Morgana	Safford
Bergen	Dibri	Issachar	Moroto	Safiyah
Berwyn	Dirk	Joakima	Mullion	Shakur
Bickel	Dixie	Joffre	Muriel	Sheehan
Boynton	Doralia	Kailah	Murray	Sheree
Branwell	Dorette	Karyn	Nandalie	Sherman
Bulooral	Dorotea	Katren	Nerida	Sheryl
Cameron	Drusilla	Kauri	Nerima	Sigmund
Carenne	Elfira	Kester	Neva	Sigurd
Cathmor	Emmelyn	Kimball	Ninette	Simpson
Cecilia	Erinn	Kineta	Niree	Siva
Cedric	Ernesto	Kinga	Norton	Somerset
Ceinlys	Erwin	Koora	Oakley	Sorrel
Celynen	Esmeralda	Krista	Oberon	Stamford
Chalmer	Eurfyl	Kumera	Odilon	Stephen
Chapin	Evan	Kylli	Othello	Sven
Charissa	Faizah	Laraine	Pandora	Sweeney
Charita	Fantine	Lareina	Parnell	Talfryn
Chastity	Faustino	Latimer	Parry	Tangwystl
Cheney	Ferenc	Laureli	Pauline	Tarleton
Chester	Gamaliel	Laurice	Peggy	Tedoroa
Chiang	Garret	Leandro	Pelagia	Teodora
Christa	Garry	Lenore	Penthea	Terrel
Ciril	Gatier	Leonard	Pepin	Thorald
Clarice	Gederts	Leonida	Philo	Townsend
Claudine	Gellies	Leonie	Phoebe	Tricia
Clemence	Genesia	Lillian	Piotr	Triska
Clinton	Gerart	Lonnie	Placido	Trixy
Clorita	Ghazi	Losaline	Pollard	Tueva
Coffey	Gibran	Maddock	Pontius	Tukaitaua
Compton	Giraud	Maggie	Price	Turner
Connie	Giselle	Mallory	Quimby	Ulrico
Cordell	Goolara	Manuelita	Radburn	Ursino
Crandell	Guillaum	Marietta	Raelene	Vanda
Crescent	Haggai	Marnie	Rebecah	Vara
Cressida	Hailey	Marnin	Reine	Warialda

Warrah	Winston	Yagoona	Yularai	Zenaida
Wilbur	Wirth	Yarraan	Yusher	Zohara
Wilmur	Woorawa	York	Zannette	

34
INTUITIVE TECHNICAL

A person with great mental discipline who has the ability to combine intuition with logic for sound decisions.

Adelpho	Cheri	Francesca	Kasper	Merry
Adelric	Chesney	Francis	Katelyn	Michaela
Akiyama	Chrystal	Frieda	Keegan	Midgee
Alfredo	Clarence	Frith	Keir	Mieke
Alkira	Clifton	Fritz	Kenton	Miklos
Amorette	Connor	Galileo	Keri	Mirella
Angelica	Corbin	Gandhi	Kerstan	Moreen
Annelise	Cordella	Gayadin	Kipp	Morina
Anthony	Cuthbert	Gladstone	Klemens	Morley
Antonina	Darrell	Gladwin	Krystal	Mozelle
Antonio	Delcine	Goldie	Kuoni	Murtagh
Archelaus	Delicia	Gwalder	Landric	Nahshon
Ariadne	Denzil	Gwydon	Laurence	Nerina
Arrian	Derek	Gwynne	Lawford	Ngutuku
Aurelius	Derry	Halifax	Leonarda	Ninian
Avara	Diamonda	Hannibal	Leopold	Nixie
Avon	Dieter	Harry	Libero	Nova
Bancroft	Dinewan	Hastings	Lilith	Nyrang
Banning	Dionetta	Hathor	Lincoln	Ondine
Beatrix	Dionne	Helmer	Lindsey	Onesimus
Beaufort	Dolores	Henry	Liv	Orazia
Bertilla	Doreen	Hermosa	Lizette	Orlando
Biagio	Dorian	Heulwen	Lleufer	Ormond
Birget	Edmondo	Honor	Lorelle	Padraic
Birin	Eithne	Hushin	Lynnette	Palmira
Bowyer	Eleanor	Iliska	Magdelen	Parnella
Branko	Elkanah	Immanuel	Maillard	Pasquette
Brenton	Embrance	Ismenia	Manfred	Paulino
Bronson	Erich	Jeremia	Marcello	Pavla
Brook	Erik	Jeroboam	Margarta	Penwyn
Cadeyrn	Erwina	Jevan	Mariane	Perez
Carleton	Eureka	Jonathon	Marino	Phedra
Carlisle	Eutyches	Kalinda	Marion	Philana
Carolyn	Evana	Karim	Matareka	Poppy
Carroll	Eystein	Karlee	Maurice	Portia
Catrine	Fanchon	Karlis	Medwenna	Pyrena
Cerwyn	Farrah	Karsten	Menchem	Pythia

Qubilah	Rosalie	Stanford	Valdus	Warren
Quennel	Rugina	Stefanie	Vamana	Weylin
Quinlan	Ryder	Stephane	Vesna	Willard
Radmilla	Rymer	Sumiko	Vic	William
Randolf	Saffron	Tangila	Vita	Winslow
Raphael	Samaritana	Teodosia	Walford	Wyborn
Redmund	Sharlyn	Terence	Walker	Wyndham
Rigby	Sierra	Terri	Wallabari	Yarramba
Roberta	Siimon	Tyrone	Waltier	Zebedee
Rodolf	Spicer	Uchtred	Wardley	Zephan
Romain	Standwood	Undurra	Warner	Zizi

35
AMBITIOUS RESOURCEFUL

This person sees possibilities for success in almost everything. Has a natural ability to use contacts for linking up and making things happen.

Adanamira	Chauncey	Dwight	Girra	Keith
Affrica	Chava	Dymock	Gloria	Kendra
Alexandra	Chemosh	Eiric	Goddard	Keren
Alistair	Cheryl	Eldrida	Gordi	Kesiah
Allirra	Cicero	Eleanora	Greer	Khalil
Annunciata	Cindie	Emeric	Gregg	Kohia
Archer	Clarabelle	Emerson	Gresham	Kylie
Arielle	Claribel	Emilie	Gunthar	Larentia
Arthfael	Clarinda	Ennion	Gwylim	Leilani
Ashford	Clemency	Eranthe	Halimeda	Leonora
Aurelie	Clova	Ericha	Hanchen	Lizzy
Azriel	Constantia	Erika	Hartley	Lombardo
Barbery	Cresswell	Ermanno	Hartmann	Lucretia
Barrie	Crosbie	Eudocie	Heidi	Lugaidh
Beckie	Cuthberta	Eugenia	Heinz	Lysander
Benedict	Cynthia	Fabrice	Hesper	Martine
Bernard	Cyrilla	Farrar	Hiawatha	Mauve
Bevan	Cythera	Felipe	Hurley	Melva
Bhaltair	Danielle	Fernand	Hypatia	Menachem
Birley	Deborah	Finian	Ignacia	Mercede
Bradburn	Denholm	Finley	Ignascha	Mercer
Brodie	Derwent	Floero	Inger	Merlin
Brough	Derwyn	Freeman	Ingmar	Milburn
Brychan	Desdemona	Fronde	Ingram	Milner
Canberra	Dietbold	Fu Chung	Irfon	Moelwyn
Carline	Dimity	Garrett	Jonquil	Monroe
Caterina	Donatello	Gaynor	Kahlil	Moreno
Cerelia	Drenka	Gerard	Karin	Myfanwy
Chantelle	Durward	Ginette	Katchen	Ninbin

Norley	Raimund	Spencer	Tilpulun	Wilder
Orion	Reamonn	Squire	Treasure	Wilmer
Painton	Reidun	Stafford	Tremain	Winsome
Parri	Romania	Steve	Ulbrecht	Wiremu
Patroclus	Rosaleen	Suvi	Ulrich	Ximenes
Pekka	Rowley	Sylgwyn	Vail	Yaminah
Pelion	Roxie	Taliesin	Vang	Yoorana
Pepilla	Ruanuku	Tapairo	Vega	Yves
Perette	Rupert	Tavis	Velda	Zabrina
Pitney	Rutger	Telford	Velma	Zahir
Prescott	Sacharissa	Teporo	Vitas	Zerelda
Preston	Scipio	Terris	Voula	Zev
Primo	Sergius	Therese	Wainbaru	
Prudent	Seymour	Theron	Warrane	
Quincy	Skipp	Thorne	Wenchi	

36
CREATIVE ARTISTIC

A person with a creative mind and an original approach to life. A lover of art and beauty often used as an outlet to express self.

Airlie	Bryony	Dunmore	Gebhard	Kalika
Alvar	Buttercup	Edeline	Gentile	Kalypso
Alvis	Capucine	Emeline	Giacomo	Kamaria
Anchitel	Carmine	Emilio	Gideon	Karina
Andreanna	Carrie	Emmaline	Giorsal	Kasmira
Angharad	Casimir	Erhard	Godwin	Keeley
Apoline	Catriona	Erline	Goliath	Keller
Aristole	Charisma	Erzebet	Gonzales	Kellie
Arval	Charley	Esterre	Gottlieb	Kenley
Augustine	Chelcie	Etienne	Grafton	Khalid
Aurelio	Chilton	Faramond	Graine	Kolora
Baradine	Christal	Farnley	Grayson	Konrad
Beatrice	Columbina	Farrell	Hardie	Koren
Beatriz	Comfort	Felicia	Hartwell	Kristal
Benedetto	Conroy	Feodor	Hashir	Labhaoise
Benedicta	Constancia	Fernanda	Henri	Lawrence
Bermillia	Coolalie	Ferry	Hermia	Leoline
Bernarda	Coralie	Filide	Hiria	Lindley
Berneen	Cristobal	Fredson	Horatia	Liorah
Blumenthal	Currita	French	Imogen	Lizanne
Brendon	Cynfor	Gabriel	Inigo	Llewelyn
Brianne	Darline	Garner	Inocenta	Lorelly
Bridey	Deidre	Gautier	Irmin	Lorenz
Bromwen	Domenic	Gavan	Jenkin	Love
Brydie	Dorice	Gearard	Julienne	Lycurgus

Lynwood	Ogier	Rayner	Stanfield	Vida
Madeline	Onorij	Redmond	Stephanos	Vlado
Magnolia	Orsino	Regina	Tennyson	Waring
Manning	Orsolija	Reilly	Thurlow	Warroo
Mareiel	Oyuki	Reinald	Tiernan	Woodley
Marietje	Patrice	Ricarda	Tiffany	Yackie
Marline	Peadair	Ringo	Toinette	Yadava
Melior	Penrod	Robine	Tychonn	Yarren
Mercedes	Perlita	Rocky	Uillioc	Yehudi
Mignon	Philetas	Rodney	Ulrika	Yoav
Miriam	Phineas	Roger	Ushnisha	Zemira
Mohammed	Phuong	Romilda	Valeda	Zenobia
Monika	Piero	Ronelle	Valetta	Zeva
Moondara	Pikuwa	Rosamond	Vance	Zilpah
Naphtali	Pixie	Royston	Vanessa	Zomelis
Napier	Prunella	Ruperta	Vanya	Zygmunt
Newbury	Queron	Salisbury	Varus	
Ngaire	Ranger	Shepley	Vasil	
Nicholas	Rayburn	Silva	Vei	
Obrien	Raymond	Sophie	Venus	

37
TRENDSETTER COMMUNICATOR
The flow of energy through written or oral skills is quite prevalent. This person will have a keen sense of what will work and be successful.

Agostino	Caprice	Derward	Gillian	Ilario
Aldrich	Carmelita	Derwin	Gillies	Indira
Alphonso	Carolina	Diomede	Gilmer	Irmina
Androcles	Casimira	Domenica	Giustina	Irwin
Aneurin	Cavell	Dove	Gordon	Ivan
Armorel	Cecilie	Edmonton	Grantham	Ives
Arvad	Ceinwen	Einfeld	Greig	Ivo
Ashburton	Charlton	Emiliana	Guiditta	Jefford
Augustino	Chuchita	Enodoch	Gustava	Jerrold
Avram	Cirilla	Enrico	Hadrian	Kamilah
Azariah	Clementia	Estavan	Halford	Karoly
Bertrand	Cleopatra	Estrelita	Happy	Killara
Birney	Conchita	Favel	Harris	Klemin
Biruni	Cradock	Fremont	Heilyn	Koleyn
Boniface	Crofton	Gabriela	Heloise	Kordula
Booreah	Darrin	Gaylord	Hercules	Kuini
Briallen	Davis	Gerber	Hilary	Kumari
Brittany	Delfine	Gerry	Hyujong	Levana
Bronwen	Dempster	Giacinta	I Chih	Liberty
Cairene	Derren	Gilbert	Ignatius	Lorenco

Lowrie	Minnette	Paavo	Ridley	Uzziah
Lucippe	Minnie	Parrell	Rinaldo	Varad
Luitpold	Mitchell	Patience	Rowandana	Venn
Lurline	Moriah	Perdita	Roxanne	Vera
Lyonelle	Murdoch	Perilla	Rudyard	Vina
Maelgwyn	Mycroft	Perry	Savage	Vitus
Mahuika	Neerim	Pieter	Serafina	Volo
Manrico	Neroli	Piper	Sharleen	Wilhelm
Marjory	Nikita	Placidia	Sirri	Yiannis
Maryanne	Nikka	Polonia	Thomasina	Yogananda
Mavis	Nimrod	Quentin	Thorpe	Yoshio
Meave	Olympia	Rachelle	Tiberia	Zachary
Melisande	Onofre	Raeline	Tiltili	Zenith
Merari	Ordelia	Raghnall	Timothea	Zenobias
Merinda	Orielda	Ragnor	Trelawny	Zinnia
Michele	Oringa	Raynor	Tristram	Zuriel
Miharo	Oxford	Rhondda	Tzigane	

38
MEDIATOR STORYTELLER

A person with a great imagination and quick wit, excellent storyteller and negotiator. Often the centre of activity.

Agamemnon	Daireen	Frick	Hotoroa	Marilyn
Amaryllis	Delight	Friend	Ihuatamai	Marmion
Aristotle	Derik	Fyodor	Ivana	Maximin
Atherton	Desiree	Ganymede	Ivy	Mildred
Avalon	Dimitra	Gennaro	Kaitlyn	Milicia
Bannerjee	Dolfine	Geraint	Kameko	Miltiades
Bardinga	Dorien	Gerwyn	Karlin	Minore
Berlinda	Dorinda	Gilberta	Katrina	Moorang
Bernice	Driscoll	Grindal	Kenwyn	Moritz
Birdie	Egidius	Grischa	Khalif	Morris
Boronia	Eirian	Guillaume	Kilian	Murphy
Bridget	Eirwen	Hamilcar	Kinsey	Napoleon
Briony	Eisenbolt	Hamilton	Kirby	Nastyenka
Cadifor	Elefreda	Hanifah	Kiri	Nerine
Chandler	Emmanuelle	Haruko	Klemmens	Noeline
Charlie	Erberto	Heather	Krystle	Noilani
Christmas	Erling	Heddwyn	Kyrena	Norbert
Cinnamon	Fairfax	Hedwig	Leonides	Okeefe
Ciorsdan	Fairlee	Helenka	Macfarlane	Orrin
Corazon	Feodosia	Hermano	Maguire	Ortensia
Corinna	Figaro	Hinemoa	Mansfield	Orva
Cromwell	Forrest	Holger	Margaret	Osvalda
Czenzi	Forster	Honorata	Margreta	Othilia

Othniel	Pierce	Rozina	Tinirau	Vonda
Parnelle	Pietro	Ruihi	Tioboid	Wenlock
Pavel	Pollyanna	Seaforth	Tremayne	Werner
Penrose	Porter	Shadrack	Tristian	Winnie
Periot	Prince	Spangler	Ulrick	Wollowra
Pernella	Quahhar	Sparrow	Vaina	Woorak
Petrina	Quinton	Spring	Vanetta	Yammacoona
Phedre	Raffalella	Syntyche	Vania	Zebadiah
Phemie	Ranier	Terentia	Varada	
Photina	Rhedyn	Thatcher	Veit	
Phyllis	Rosalind	Timothy	Vijo	

39
COMPOSED DISCRIMINATING

A reserved person, often thought of as shy, which they are not. Likes the finer things in life. Excels when encouraged.

Adolfine	Confucius	Florian	Koppel	Perpetua
Alexander	Constantin	Fonzie	Kristy	Pollock
Alexandre	Coralice	Francesco	Kurrawa	Prentiss
Andromeda	Crisiant	Freedom	Kyril	Prewitt
Aophonse	Cristian	George	Leonardo	Querida
Ariki	Cristina	Giocobo	Leonore	Radford
Assumption	Cyrille	Giraldo	Levi	Reynold
Bardick	Daffodil	Gottrid	Llewellyn	Ricky
Berthold	Dakini	Griselda	Loring	Rieke
Bevis	Darianne	Gunther	Magdelene	Roberto
Bilhilda	Davey	Gurion	Marianne	Ronnie
Bootoolga	Davita	Gwyneth	Markku	Rozelle
Bosworth	Demetria	Hanford	Mayfield	Sachiko
Bozidar	Derryn	Hanraoi	Mehitabel	Savina
Britney	Dionnetta	Hariclea	Merryn	Schuyler
Bronwyn	Doongara	Harika	Mickey	Seirian
Brooke	Drummond	Helier	Mirko	Sharron
Byrger	Eanruig	Iolanthe	Morrell	Sherry
Caronwen	Egerton	Jeffery	Mowantyi	Sidonie
Catharina	Eirig	Jeffrey	Nathaniel	Sigrid
Celestino	Eisenbart	Jeronim	Nikolaus	Simonette
Cerilia	Eleanore	Jevon	Norris	Sponner
Charity	Eugenie	Kamini	Norwin	Stephania
Charleen	Evart	Karri	Octave	Sybillie
Charlotte	Evita	Katarina	Ophelia	Templeton
Cherie	Farrer	Kenyon	Orazio	Thankful
Chloris	Ferris	Kirra	Orpheus	Trahern
Christos	Filipe	Kirsty	Palmiro	Trinette
Cirilo	Fleming	Kliment	Paramahansa	Tristanne

Tutanekai	Vidal	Voleta	Warreen	Woorail
Vallia	Vilma	Waitangi	Warrina	Wundurra
Vallis	Vito	Warrack	Windsor	Ziv

40
SOLID RATIONAL
These people are often set in their ways. Require a home base. Down-to-earth persons who are rational and resist change.

Alver	Devota	Gribbon	Kristel	Reynard
Alvin	Didier	Guilbert	Kristle	Riobard
Antigone	Dolorita	Harmony	Krysten	Ripley
Archibald	Dominic	Heathcote	Lloydice	Rodger
Aristocles	Dorryn	Herbert	Lorelei	Rodolfo
Avenall	Elizabella	Hikka	Lourenco	Rorke
Beatriks	Elvis	Hrisoula	Makitaka	Rudolph
Bernadette	Emmeline	Iachimo	Menachin	Sharolyn
Bertilia	Engelina	Ignacio	Merv	Sinclair
Birwain	Engracia	Ihakara	Methuselah	Sophocles
Boondoon	Enrika	Ingemar	Michelle	Steven
Brigid	Eugenio	Innocent	Mitiaro	Stratford
Brinley	Fairley	Ishmawil	Monique	Terrill
Budgeree	Falkner	Istvan	Ngahere	Thorley
Celandine	Ferrars	Kakuei	Ngoc Nhan	Tirrell
Charmian	Fifine	Kataraina	Nicodemus	Torrance
Cheiro	Finnian	Kathleen	Nicolette	Trixie
Cherise	Folker	Katinka	Oconnor	Urvan
Christel	Fortunato	Kennard	Orford	Vadim
Cindylou	Francois	Kepler	Peninah	Valmai
Clorinda	Fremantle	Kerill	Peronel	Veleda
Colinette	Gardner	Kermit	Pipipa	Verla
Columbine	Garrie	Khoung	Prahnee	Visant
Constantina	Georges	Kieran	Puillian	Wirake
Cordelia	Geremia	Kiki	Queenie	Wolfgang
Corydon	Germain	Kinnia	Quillam	Wright
Courtney	Gershom	Kinsie	Quiller	Zerlina
Cytherea	Gislaine	Kirk	Quincey	Ziva
David	Gorky	Kirstel	Radinka	Zuleika
Devi	Grazina	Kitri	Rewuri	

41
INGENIOUS ENERGETIC
An extremely resourceful person capable of making something from seemingly nothing. Excels under pressure and in impromptu situations.

Albertine	Courtenay	Herberta	Meridee	Sterling
Alfonsine	Cyprian	Herrod	Mikko	Sutherland
Alvina	Davida	Hiriwa	Milford	Tekooti
Amerigo	Davin	Horatio	Mirria	Theodora
Apollonia	Derrin	Hortense	Modestine	Tirranna
Aristides	Dietbrand	Ichibod	Mordecai	Toshiro
Avir	Digger	Imogene	Nicander	Turlough
Benedicto	Domingo	Iorwyn	Nicomede	Ulpirra
Berghetta	Dominica	Irva	Norwood	Vari
Bernardo	Dorothea	Ivar	Ohini	Varuna
Bernhart	Esperance	Iven	Olympie	Verda
Bilyarra	Essington	Ivetta	Orchio	Vere
Bradford	Estevan	Jakov	Oroiti	Vern
Brigida	Evette	Jedidiah	Orval	Vine
Brinsley	Fernando	Jovita	Patricia	Viola
Cairine	Fielder	Kandelka	Phaedora	Vira
Calpurnia	Flaherty	Kedric	Prudence	Wadsworth
Cardinia	Fletcher	Kemper	Quiric	Wendelin
Carnation	Gabriele	Kenneth	Raphaeia	Whitney
Caroline	Gellimar	Kerry	Reinwald	Wilfred
Cavill	Gerardo	Killian	Rhiain	Winchell
Cherry	Gerhart	Kimiya	Ricardo	Wirruna
Christanta	Gershon	Kinnell	Riva	Woodrow
Constancio	Gilroy	Kirli	Roarke	Yarrawah
Cornelia	Gustave	Langford	Rodhlann	Zacharias
Cornelis	Halfrida	Lavina	Rurik	Zofeyah
Cornish	Harcourt	Madeleine	Snowhite	

42
EMOTIONAL TRADITIONAL

A sensitive person who is not afraid to show emotions. Needs tradition and ritual in their life to feel normal.

Albertino	Demetrius	Flavia	Gwynllyn	Kermadec
Aldridge	Dimiter	Flinders	Hartigan	Kerstin
Ambrosine	Dorothy	Florence	Heiki	Keziah
Amhlaoibh	Dorrie	Florenz	Hermando	Kirsten
Antoinette	Durrebar	Garibaldo	Herschel	Knight
Arvis	Ellsworth	Garnock	Ibrahim	Koenraad
Ashleigh	Elridge	Ginger	Indrani	Kristen
Astrophel	Esperanza	Goodwin	Jeremiah	Kumbelin
Berngard	Euphemia	Goonagulla	Kaliope	Lorenzo
Clive	Evadne	Griston	Katrine	Macharios
Corinne	Fairlie	Guglielma	Keiko	Makarios
Cypriana	Ferguson	Guistino	Kennedy	Margery
Davina	Finigan	Gwai Neebu	Kereru	Margrete

Melbourne	Peronne	Rizpah	Stavros	Ville
Merrill	Polyzena	Rochelle	Svein	Vitale
Nerva	Queanbeyan	Rosemary	Thank Xuan	Warburton
Nicomedes	Quigley	Seiriol	Theodosia	Whistler
Parker	Quintina	Serafino	Tierney	Wilfreda
Parkin	Raleigh	Sheridan	Vachel	Wilkin
Patrick	Rawiri	Sherwin	Valek	Wynford
Pericles	Reinaldo	Shirley	Valora	Yangoora
Peridot	Rhianne	Silvana	Vanni	Yooralia
Pernelle	Rhodeia	Sirkka	Verna	

43
RESEARCHER SECRETIVE

A person interested in history, literature or anything from the past. Strong-willed, creative, has great inner control.

Adrienne	Emmeric	Harriet	Millicent	Sylvia
Aineislis	Engelbert	Hernando	Minkie	Tewahoroa
Bennelong	Ephraim	Herzog	Muirhead	Thiewie
Berenice	Errki	Hyacinth	Nakkare	Thorbert
Bernstein	Florinda	Ingrid	Novia	Thornton
Bevin	Francisco	Irmgard	Omphalie	Trinity
Boleslav	Gerhard	Isidore	Ottavia	Uldricks
Britannia	Gerlinda	Ivanna	Penelope	Vaino
Calvin	Gerritt	Ivka	Philip	Vashti
Cellandine	Gilberto	Izydor	Randolph	Vasilos
Charline	Gilbrid	Jacqueline	Reginald	Vasily
Cheyenne	Gilling	Jarvis	Rhonwen	Vidya
Chiquita	Gilmore	Jennyfer	Richard	Vilem
Chriselda	Giselbert	Kaikasi	Richette	Vogel
Christabel	Giuliano	Katerina	Richie	Warwick
Covey	Gonzalez	Kathryn	Riordan	Weeronga
Crawford	Granger	Kerri	Robinson	Wilkins
Crispin	Gregor	Kogarah	Rodolph	Winfred
Devnet	Grimaldo	Lionardo	Sapphira	Xaver
Eckhardt	Guthrie	Margarita	Snowdrop	Yvette
Eirik	Gwenllian	Marigold	Stephanie	Zakelina
Eliphalet	Gyorgy	Mereki	Swithbert	
Elizabeth	Harmonia	Miguelita	Sylvanus	

44
ARCHITECT ALCHEMIST

A master energy that gives power to the person to build and make things happen relatively easily. Has a magnetic personality.

Abernethy	leonore	Gretchen	Lindberg	Ridgley
Ackerley	Eliezer	Griswold	Livia	Sauveur
Agathenor	Elvin	Guiseppe	Lockwood	Saville
Alexandria	Engelberta	Harriot	Loughlin	Sevilla
Ativee	Enrique	Havgan	Malvin	Sherwood
Avery	Euchario	Henriot	Marjorie	Stiven
Avril	Euphrasia	Hepetipa	Maurizia	Tepotatango
Beauvais	Felicity	Hilaire	Melvia	Thorburn
Bridgid	Fengshui	Hoibeard	Muralappi	Travis
Brunhilda	Fridmund	Honoria	Nunkalowe	Tryphena
Chadwick	Fulvia	Hyacintha	Octavia	Valence
Charleene	Gabrielle	Jaroslav	Paavali	Valeska
Chemarin	Gallagher	Jefferson	Perrin	Vanora
Clairmond	Garfield	Karmein	Philantha	Vassily
Clovis	Garve	Karrin	Philaret	Vellamo
Constantine	Gauthier	Kasimir	Phillida	Verban
Cornelius	Gavin	Kerwin	Pierre	Vicar
Crispian	Georgia	Kinnard	Pomeroy	Vince
Crispina	Gertrude	Konstancia	Prioska	Volante
Derryth	Giocopo	Konstanze	Prosper	Wahleroa
Dervla	Giuseppe	Korong	Rebekka	Warranunna
Donoghue	Godfrey	Krishna	Riccardo	Worippa
Ebenezer	Goraidh	Kristof	Richenda	Zerlinda

45
DEDICATED BENEVOLENT

A person who is completely unique and uncompromising. They let nothing get in the way once they are convinced of something.

Andriessen	Dionysius	Geneva	Kasimira	Nunkumbil
Bailintin	Divis	Geordie	Katarzyna	Olive
Bernadine	Doralicia	Germaine	Keifer	Panayiotos
Brigitte	Dorothee	Ginsberg	Koolyoo	Penrith
Bringham	Egidion	Godafrey	Krisian	Pharamond
Brionie	Elvina	Gualterio	Labhruinn	Philbert
Carrick	Emerentia	Gwendolen	Lakkari	Pierina
Ceridwen	Enright	Gwynfor	Leighton	Pirrit
Charmaine	Erskine	Harried	Levina	Prentice
Cheiron	Eurydice	Hermine	Lorimer	Priscilla
Chevy	Fabrician	Ignazio	Malvina	Rafferty
Cornelie	Farquhar	Ivette	Mikhail	Rhidian
Culver	Flavius	Jarvey	Mirrin	Rhodope
Cyndeyrn	Floranthe	Jennifer	Moireach	Rhydwyn
Deirdre	Florimel	Jeromino	Myimbarr	Richelle
Demetrios	Gabriello	Kaooroo	Nehemiah	Rockwell
Devin	Garnier	Karolina	Nikki	Salvator

Sedgwick	Thank Danh	Valenty	Wargarang	Yirki
Sigfrid	Theodore	Valmond	Wilfrid	Yooneeara
Silvanus	Theodosius	Vasili	Wirinun	Yorick
Silvia	Trahaiarn	Vedette	Woorree	
Stephenson	Urvasi	Vonny	Yehoshafat	

46
AFFLUENT RESOLUTE

These people appear well-to-do, often attracting abundance. They stand up for themselves, having the courage of convictions of self and others.

Andronicus	Dover	Kingdom	Nevin	Seraphina
Arvin	Ernestine	Kingston	Pekeri	Sherlock
Beauregard	Ezekiel	Kirstie	Peospero	Sperling
Burleigh	Frankie	Kirstin	Petronella	Varden
Carmichael	Goonaroo	Kourapapa	Philberta	Vaughn
Christie	Gweneira	Krister	Philiman	Venance
Clementine	Helianthe	Kristin	Puriri	Verne
Clifford	Henrietta	Margriet	Quiteria	Verra
Concordia	Hilliard	Mei Kuei	Radcliffe	Virna
Cornelio	Humphry	Melvyn	Ragnhild	Vychan
Curringa	Ivor	Meredith	Roderica	Warringa
Delphine	Izidora	Mikhaila	Rudiger	Wirrin
Democritus	Kathrina	Naliandrah	Ruprecht	

47
TENACITY STUDENT

A hard working person who perseveres and is most productive when reaching for a goal or dream. The perpetual student, always learning.

Arlington	Elgiva	Inglebert	Onofredo	Valery
Arnoldine	Enriqueta	Javier	Onofrio	Valgard
Avenida	Evelyn	Jervis	Orrick	Valonia
Berenger	Fabrienne	Josephine	Parthenia	Varian
Beresford	Federico	Keokuk	Philemon	Varina
Berkeley	Filippo	Kindilan	Quarrallia	Vaschka
Berrigan	Fiorello	Kirri	Quirinus	Vassilia
Berrilee	Fitzroy	Konstantin	Rainier	Vaughan
Brockwell	Flavian	Kristina	Rhianwen	Ventura
Byrnhild	Flavio	Laibrook	Rhianydd	Verena
Carinthia	Franklyn	Lorraine	Salvador	Violet
Catherine	Galvin	Margarite	Sapphire	Weaver
Charitina	Gianinno	Melchoir	Sherrill	Wentworth
Christian	Gifford	Michelina	Subrahmanyan	Zippora
Christina	Guglielmo	Mireille	Sullivan	Zoroaster
Conradine	Gwendolyn	Nunkeri	Tourmaline	
Edwardine	Iacovo	Octavius	Traviata	

48
ASTUTE ACHIEVER

This person's approach is in an orderly manner, precise and executed with power. Compelled to achieve at almost any cost.

Ainsleigh	Ferdinand	Jehoshaphat	Pulcheria	Verge
Averell	Fielding	Kerrie	Rhiannon	Verita
Brighid	Friedmann	Kilkie	Rhodanthe	Verona
Broughton	Gallipoli	Kingsley	Richmond	Vinita
Christobel	Georgette	Kokomis	Riordon	Vinny
Clover	Geraldine	Loveday	Rochester	Vinson
Conchubhar	Given	Ludvig	Seville	Volney
Delvin	Habakkuk	Melvin	Sylvain	Xenophon
Evanthe	Harrison	Mortimer	Tangerine	Yoshiko
Evonne	Hibernia	Octavie	Valentia	Zachariah
Farleigh	Hyacinthe	Philomena	Verdun	Zygfryd

49
VIRTUOUS COOPERATIVE

A person with high integrity who cannot understand pettiness. Takes pride in being cooperative. Works well with groups and associations.

Alexandrina	Enrichetta	Karoline	Philothea	Thimothee
Archimedes	Ferninand	Klinger	Pythagoras	Travers
Averil	Franklin	Kornelia	Rayleigh	Uggieri
Calphurnia	Gardiner	Laverty	Rikki	Valdemar
Carver	Garrick	Macpherson	Rosemarie	Venetia
Cherilyn	Godiva	Miloslav	Silver	Venice
Crighton	Grunhilda	Morrison	Sylvania	Verbena
Delvene	Guillermo	Murrumbung	Teauotangaroa	Wakefield
Dietrich	Hiroko	Norvall	Thank Tuyen	Washington
Donovan	Iskender	Orinthia	Themistocles	
Elvira'	Ivanka	Pembroke	Theophila	

50
LIBERATED ACTIVE

This person needs freedom, often evading responsibility. Always in motion, attracting attention wherever they go.

Aveline	Evelina	Georgios	Hildegard	Kathrine
Benedictina	Everett	Gervase	Hilderic	Kimberly
Derrick	Evva	Gottfried	Hiroshi	Koiranah
Eremelinda	Frederic	Gregory	Hong Hgoc	Laverne
Eveleen	Frenchie	Herminia	Ingeborg	Lavinia

Maighdlin	Petronilla	Sedgewick	Vaslav	Withinka
Marvin	Philipp	Siegfrid	Vespera	Wyterrica
Merrilees	Primrose	Teodorico	Vigil	Xavery
Narbethong	Reinhard	Valborg	Violetta	Yaroslav
Olivia	Ringbalin	Valeria	Wellington	Yung Chih
Papatuanuki	Salvatore	Valori	Whitaker	Yvonne

51
INDEPENDENT AUTHORITY

Authority figures who look for truth in all they come into contact with. Must have freedom to let independent nature come through, which often conflicts with home and family needs.

Amirov	Garvey	Iverna	Mokoiro	Vicente
Aphrodite	Gavril	Katharine	Morven	Victor
Bartholomew	Geoffrey	Katherina	Orithyia	Villette
Christabelle	Geronimo	Katimarie	Orvin	Vincent
Christine	Gilchrist	Kinsford	Philemina	Winthrop
Conception	Griffin	Kirilly	Philippa	Wivina
Diedrik	Heathcliff	Krispin	Raoghnailt	Yoshishisa
Dixiebelle	Hermione	Kristine	Spofforth	Yoyangamalde
Evander	Hoang Hgoc	Mackenzie	Tuulikki	Zedekiah
Federigo	Humphrey	Mariequita	Valarian	
Fitzhugh	Indrikus	Maximilian	Valborga	
Frederica	Ivanku	Micheline	Velika	

52
INVENTIVE SPECULATIVE

A person with insight and ideas that are often far ahead of their time. Always open, uses the old to establish the new, takes chances.

Christiane	Harvey	Nuvarahu	Theophania	Wilhelmina
Christobella	Kevin	Remington	Trygve	Winchester
Chrysander	Kornelius	Ruaidhri	Vaclav	Winifred
Clavier	Mervyn	Sigourney	Vernon	Xavier
Concepcion	Minamberang	Sophronia	Vicky	Zechariah
Devaki	Neville	Theodoric	Whiangaroa	Zephaniah

53
COMPETITOR ENTERPRISING

A creative person with a fine-tuned intellect who thrives on competition. Often a risk-taker who enjoys a challenge.

Alexandrine	Evaristus	Heikki	Millington	Velko
Bainbridge	Garvin	Ivory	Pinterry	Verbina
Beverly	Gieorgia	Kenrick	Sigvard	Verney
Bhagavati	Giorgio	Kirilyn	Solveig	Willoughby
Christianna	Girvan	Kurmoonah	Tikvah	Xaviera
Delvine	Gregoria	Massimiliano	Trevor	
Dominique	Harkishan	Mercurino	Valentina	

54
OBSERVER UNORTHODOX

These people are often misunderstood in their quest to be free. Often referred to as Bohemian. They appear to be the observers of the world, achieving without being obvious.

Aviv	Guiseppina	Lavender	Verity	Wollondilly
Constitucion	Henrick	Marguerite	Veve	Zavier
Creighton	Hoireabard	Maximillian	Vicki	Zivian
Eveline	Ihorangi	Melville	Vilhelm	
Fitzgerald	Irvin	Mervin	Virdis	
Gervais	Ivanjuscha	Oliver	Viva	
Govinda	Kiritin	Valerie	Wirrilar	

55
PIONEER ENTREPRENEUR

This is a master energy vibration that gives the person a guiding force to lead the way with new ideas. Natural administrator with the ability to handle several things at the same time.

Agrippina	Frobisher	Kimberley	Pickford	Venedict
Aviva	Gheorghe	Maximilien	Ruggiero	Vinnie
Christinha	Herewini	Millemurro	Siegfried	Yulwirree
Evangelos	Hezekiah	Minerva	Sylvester	Yung Chiang
Everard	Hildegarde	Miroslav	Valerian	Zephirah
Fleurdelice	Katherine	Montgomery	Valerio	
Frankfort	Kelvin	Philippe	Varick	

56
AMBASSADOR JUDGE

A person with good intuition and insight who can assist others to their right path or decision. Can see both sides of a situation, which makes for an excellent judge.

Berringar	Frederico	Heinrich	Robindalgar	Volker
Beverlee	Giovanna	Kurnkuni	Roderick	Zenovia
Dimitiris	Griffith	Norvin	Verrell	
Eleutherios	Guillelmine	Peregrin	Vidonia	

57
IMAGINATIVE ADAPTABLE

This person has a lot of energy that is directed at new and better ways to do things. Ideas often come faster than they can be implemented. Must take care not to over-extend.

Benvenura	Mairghread	Rheinhold	Valentine
Gioacchino	Natividad	Silvester	Waverley
Kendrick	Orville	Thanh Phong	Wirreecoo
Kereteki	Peregrina	Triantafilia	Xaverie

58
EXPLORER METHODICAL

A born systems expert. Not easily distracted. Experimental by nature, will try new things in the name of perfection.

Beverley	Frederik	Grover	Lillipilli	Xaviero
Broderick	Ginevra	Hippocrates	Merivale	
Christofer	Goldsworthy	Kentigern	Murrembooee	
Everlida	Gregorio	Kristofer	Persephone	

59
ADVENTUROUS FASCINATING

Fascinating people whose sense of adventure seems to take them from one situation to another. The need to travel seems overwhelming.

Coventry	Kinnereth	Trevelyan	Viktor
Havelock	Ludovika	Valmiki	Violinda
Irvine	Percival	Velvet	Virgil

60
CONSULTANT SENSITIVE

Extremely sensitive people who surround themselves with family, friends and home matters. Often the wise counsel who brings balance.

Beverlie	Kimbereley	Verrill	Violinna	Wainwright
Gothfraidh	Veronica	Vigilia	Vittoria	

61
PERCEPTIVE MAVERICK

A rational yet perceptive person who dislikes conformity. Seldom expresses feelings openly, uses quiet power.

Bedevire	Kirkwood	Pirramurar	Victoria
Frederick	Ogilvie	Rutherford	Vincentia
Irving	Peregrine	Varnava	Vladimir

62
ADMINISTRATOR HONEST

This person has the foresight to plan and implement successfully, enjoys directing. Very straightforward and fair.

Lirralirra	Vevila	Vikki	Warriwillah	Wilberforce
Norville				

63
FLEXIBLE ALTRUISTIC

A deep-feeling person with a big heart who is always ready to lend a helping hand or sympathetic ear. Able to adapt to almost any situation with creative flair.

Everhard	Olivier	Vevette	Viking	Viridis

64
DISTINGUISHED NOTORIOUS

Persons with this energy can have honours come to them as they are driven to help and are often pillars of the community. Everyone seems to know them.

Christoffer	Granville	Veikko	Vevina	Virgile
Giovanni				

65
INSPIRATIONAL SUPPORTER

A compassionate person who rallies to many causes, often giving inspiration. May be called upon to act as messenger or arbitrator.

Euloowirree   Philadelphia   Varvara   Victorie   Vittorio
Kerekori

66
HEALER UPLIFTER

A master energy vibration that uplifts others, as this person has a natural ability to tune into others' feelings and needs. Must learn to give while separating self from others' problems.

Vladislav

67
REALIST LOGICAL

These people are aware of their capabilities and know how to juggle responsiblity with self-needs. Normally operate from a logical point of view.

Christopher   Hargrove   Ngaroariki   Primavera   Veloneika
Evangeline   Kristopher

68
RESILIENT ENTHUSIAST

A person who rolls with the punches of life, usually coming out on top. Has zeal and good outlook, eager to forge ahead where others fear.

Christophera   Koninderie   Veronika   Vivian

69
COMPOSED PRECISE

A peaceful level-headed person who approaches life in an organised, precise manner. Uncanny ability to put others at ease. Enjoys quiet familiar surroundings where best results are achieved.

Vilhelmina   Virgilia   Viviana

70
GENIUS ECCENTRIC

A person with a high degree of intelligence and talent. Often misunderstood, with strange habits and traits. Seems to be on a different wavelength. Finds it hard to express feelings to others.

Grosvenor   Guinevere

71
DEPENDABLE VISIONARY

A quiet achiever who is reliable and trustworthy. A visionary can foresee events before they happen; must learn to trust insights.

Vekoslav   Virginia

72
CONVENTIONAL CONSTRUCTIVE

A person with high ideals and standards who plans and executes with precision. Often completes what was left undone by others.

Veronique   Vivien   Weringerong   Wurrawilberoo

73
POETIC MYSTICAL

A seemingly dreamy loner with a creative flair for the unusual; often a poet or philosopher. In tune when flowing from inner wisdom. Often misunderstood or before their time.

74
VIRTUOUS ANALYTICAL

A candid person, often lacking in tact. Can be extremely analytical; often over-critical. Has a magnetic attraction — people either love or dislike this person. Honours are often bestowed on them.

Livingstone   Orvokki

75
PROLIFIC PERSISTENT

A quick thinker who puts ideas into tangible works, making things happen. Has the drive and tenacity to see things through.

Beverleigh   Virginie

76
CONFORMIST SINCERE

An adaptable person who generally follows rather than leads. Genuine in approach, often overworked, must learn to balance work with leisure time.

Berrookboorn

77
RESTORER UNCONVENTIONAL

A master energy that is gifted in natural health or the healing field. Appears eccentric, gravitates to unconventional lifestyle. Often secretive in approach to restoration remedies.

78
INSTINCTIVE WISDOM

These people are wise beyond their years, having the natural ability to combine logic with intuition. Often involved with associations or groups in consultancy position.

79
PRINCIPLED SACRIFICING

A person with strong principles, often on a mission. The intellect seems to rule the emotions. Willing to make sacrifices for the good of others, can become a martyr.

80
PROSPEROUS SELF-RELIANT

Self disciplined and capable of all they set out to do. Often prosperous, they seem to accumulate things and people. Must take care not to become hoarders.

81
PRAGMATIC SENSIBLE
A level-headed person who gives without thought and receives without forgetting. Calm and in control, has ability to handle affairs and people with practical approach.

82
GUIDE SUPPORTIVE
An authority figure who keeps up-to-date and informed. Enjoys assisting others with this information. Others often seek out this knowledge.

Vivienne

83
DIPLOMAT ORATOR
A person with the ability to be persuasive and helpful, using a natural sense of protocol. A gifted speaker, can hold an audience with this ability.

84
PROGRESSIVE RELIABLE
A reliable manager, often an executive, capable of handling authority and power in a progressive manner. You can always count on these people to be there for their friends.

85
INTEGRITY DISCIPLINARIAN
A person who is extremely disciplined with self and those around them. Cannot tolerate dishonesty and always operates by the book.

Genevieve

86
EFFICIENT MAGNETIC
A person with a lot of energy. Has the power of attraction. Adaptable and efficient at what they set out to do, these people dislike being led.

Christopherine

87
RESPECTABLE INFLUENTIAL

A well-thought-of person who brings out the best in others. Often has noble ideas but can lack follow-through.

88
CRUSADER PERFECTIONIST

A master energy that gives this person inner wisdom with a desire to revolutionise the world. A perfectionist by nature, needs to balance material with spiritual to achieve often lofty goals. Often nervous and over-critical.

89
ADVISER MOTIVATOR

This person is drawn to help guide others. Often inspirational and motivational, can sense the constructive path.

90
STABLE GUARDIAN

A person who seems secure and stable, often defending and helping others. Thought of as the big brother or sister to others. Has uncanny way of being there when needed.

91
PATHFINDER MANAGER

These people are drawn to issues regarding their surroundings, often taking the initiative. Natural managerial abilities to implement new methods to help mankind.

92
PEACEMAKER PHILANTHROPIC

A humanitarian who needs peace at all costs. A benevolent nature, never at a loss for companions and friends. Must have quiet time to rest and contemplate.

93
CAPTIVATING PROPHETIC

Persons with broad visions, often instinctively knowing what will work and what to do. Have a mysterious captivating charm about them that fascinates others.

94
MASTERMIND DEXTERITY
A clever person who knows how to engineer things into workable plans. Has a natural ability to develop and make things in skilfull fashion.

95
SPONTANEOUS WANDERER
This person has gypsy tendencies. Uses intuition or gut feelings when making decisions. Has a real need for freedom which must be balanced with the love of people.

96
EDUCATOR BENEFACTOR
A natural teacher who uses gifts of compassion and love in a selfless manner. Will be drawn to join in with groups and associations. Must use balance not to become used.

97
PHILOSOPHER CONTEMPLATOR
A perceptive and wise person who is often contemplative or dreamy and slow to react. Often removes self from the outside world as needs to be alone to formulate thoughts into productive information.

98
SUBTLE PROFICIENT
These people are subtle or suggestive in their dealings with others. Often knowing what they want, they go about obtaining it in a skilful manner. They dislike leaving things undone or unattended.

99
ALTRUISTIC GURU
A master energy that brings visionary abilities. Prophetic in word and expression, these people strive to help others by example and leading the way.

8 Index of Names

Although this listing indicates a gender preference after each name (F = female, M = male, B = both), it is important to realise that any name could be used for either sex as the interpretations are universal.

These names are generally used as first and middle names. Last names (surnames, family names) will have to be constructed using the alphanumeric conversion grid.

Aaron	22	M	Abessa	11	F	Adabelle	24	F
Abadi	17	M	Abigael	28	F	Adah	14	F
Abadie	22	F	Abigail	32	F	Adair	24	M
Abba	6	B	Abner	22	M	Adal	9	F
Abbas	7	M	Abrabella	27	F	Adalard	23	M
Abbey	17	F	Abraham	26	M	Adalia	19	F
Abbot	13	M	Abram	17	M	Adam	10	M
Abbott	15	M	Abu	6	M	Adama	11	F
Abby	12	F	Acacia	18	F	Adamina	25	F
Abdarah	26	M	Ace	9	M	Adaminah	33	F
Abduh	18	M	Achill	27	M	Adan	11	M
Abdul	13	M	Achilla	28	F	Adanamira	35	F
Abdullah	25	M	Achille	32	M	Adar	15	B
Abe	8	M	Achilles	33	M	Addala	14	F
Abel	11	M	Acima	18	F	Addis	19	M
Abelard	25	M	Ackerley	44	M	Addison	30	M
Abernethy	44	M	Ada	6	F	Adela	14	F

Adelaide	32	F	Agathon	30	M	Alair	23	M
Adelbert	31	M	Agato	17	M	Alam	9	M
Adelberta	32	F	Agia	18	F	Alameda	19	F
Adele	18	F	Agilus	24	M	Alan	10	M
Adelina	28	F	Agipatus	31	M	Alana	11	F
Adelinda	32	F	Aglia	21	F	Alanna	16	F
Adeline	32	F	Agnas	15	F	Alard	18	M
Adelle	21	F	Agnes	19	F	Alaric	26	M
Adelpha	29	F	Agnessa	21	F	Alasdair	29	M
Adelpho	34	M	Agostina	32	F	Alart	16	M
Adelric	34	M	Agostino	37	M	Alasdair	29	M
Aden	15	M	Agrippina	55	F	Alastair	27	M
Aderyn	31	F	Ahearn	29	M	Alaster	22	M
Adila	18	F	Ahern	28	M	Alastor	23	M
Adina	20	F	Ahmad	18	M	Alaura	18	F
Adler	22	M	Ahmed	22	M	Alba	7	B
Adley	20	M	Ahren	28	M	Albacett	19	M
Adolf	20	M	Aida	15	F	Alban	12	M
Adolfine	39	F	Aidan	20	M	Alben	16	M
Adolph	29	M	Aideen	29	F	Albert	22	M
Adon	16	M	Aiden	24	M	Alberta	23	F
Adoni	25	M	Aidhan	28	M	Albertine	41	F
Adonia	26	F	Aigneis	28	F	Albertino	42	M
Adonis	26	M	Aikane	32	M	Alberto	28	M
Adora	21	F	Aileen	28	F	Albion	26	M
Adoree	30	F	Ailie	27	F	Albret	22	M
Adrana	21	F	Ailsa	15	F	Alcina	22	F
Adria	24	F	Aime	19	F	Alcott	17	M
Adrian	29	M	Aimee	24	F	Alda	9	F
Adriana	30	F	Aine	20	F	Aldabella	23	F
Adriel	31	M	Aineislis	43	M	Alden	18	M
Adrien	33	M	Ainslea	25	F	Alder	22	M
Adrienne	43	F	Ainslee	29	F	Aldis	18	M
Adrine	33	F	Ainsleigh	48	F	Aldo	14	M
Aeneas	18	M	Ainsley	31	B	Aldous	18	M
Afan	13	M	Ainslie	33	M	Aldred	26	M
Affrica	35	F	Airlie	36	F	Aldrich	37	M
Afic	19	F	Ajax	9	M	Aldridge	42	M
Afra	17	F	Akala	17	F	Aldwin	27	M
Agale	17	F	Akashi	31	F	Alec	12	M
Agamemnon	38	M	Akim	25	M	Aleda	14	F
Agapa	17	F	Akira	31	M	Alejandra	30	F
Agape	21	F	Akiyama	34	M	Alena	15	F
Agata	12	F	Akuna	21	F	Alester	26	M
Agatha	20	F	Akyssha	30	F	Aleta	12	F
Agathe	24	F	Aladdin	27	M	Alethea	25	F
Agathenor	44	M	Alain	19	M	Alex	15	B
Agatho	25	M	Alaine	24	F	Alexa	16	F

Alexander	39	M	Alonzo	29	M	Ambler	24	M
Alexandra	35	F	Aloysius	31	M	Ambrose	28	F
Alexandre	39	M	Alpha	20	F	Ambrosine	42	F
Alexandria	44	F	Alpheus	28	M	Amelia	23	F
Alexandrina	49	F	Alphonse	36	M	Amelina	28	F
Alexandrine	53	F	Alphonso	37	M	Amelinda	32	F
Alexia	25	F	Alred	22	M	America	32	F
Alexis	25	B	Alroy	26	M	Amerigo	41	M
Alfonsa	23	F	Alston	18	M	Amery	26	M
Alfonsine	41	F	Alter	20	M	Amethyst	30	F
Alfonso	28	M	Althea	20	F	Amfrid	33	M
Alfred	28	M	Alton	17	M	Amhlaoibh	42	M
Alfreda	29	F	Alun	12	M	Amico	23	M
Alfredo	34	M	Alva	27	B	Amida	19	M
Algar	21	M	Alvar	36	M	Amie	19	F
Alger	25	M	Alver	40	M	Amin	19	M
Ali	13	B	Alvin	40	M	Amir	23	M
Alice	21	F	Alvina	41	F	Amirov	51	M
Alicia	26	F	Alvis	36	M	Amity	23	F
Alie	18	F	Alwin	23	B	Ammon	20	M
Alisa	15	F	Alwyn	21	B	Amnon	21	M
Alisha	23	F	Alys	12	F	Amon	16	M
Alison	25	F	Alysia	22	F	Amorette	34	F
Alisson	26	F	Alyson	23	F	Amorita	32	F
Alistair	35	M	Alyssa	14	F	Amory	27	M
Alister	30	M	Alyssha	22	F	Amos	12	M
Alix	19	F	Alyx	17	M	Amparo	28	M
Alkira	34	F	Amadea	16	F	Amund	17	M
Allambee	24	M	Amadeus	19	M	Amy	12	F
Allan	13	M	Amador	25	M	Amyntas	21	M
Allanah	22	F	Amahl	17	M	Ana	7	F
Allard	21	M	Amalia	19	F	Anais	17	F
Allegra	29	F	Amalie	23	F	Ananda	17	M
Allen	17	M	Amalthea	25	F	Ananias	23	M
Alleyne	29	M	Amama	11	M	Anarawd	26	M
Allie	21	F	Amanda	16	F	Anaru	19	M
Allirra	35	F	Amandus	19	M	Anastasia	22	F
Allison	28	F	Amara	16	F	Anastasie	26	F
Allunga	23	M	Amarantha	32	F	Anastatius	26	M
Allyn	19	M	Amarina	30	F	Anata	10	F
Allyson	26	F	Amaris	25	F	Anatole	23	M
Alma	9	F	Amaryllis	38	F	Ancel	17	M
Almadine	32	F	Amasa	8	M	Anchitel	36	M
Almena	19	F	Amat	8	M	Ancia	19	F
Almond	23	F	Amata	9	F	Ancika	30	F
Aloha	19	F	Amba	8	F	Anders	25	M
Aloisia	30	F	Ambar	17	F	Andie	24	F
Alon	15	M	Amber	21	F	Andras	21	M

Andre	24	M	Anselm	19	M	Arbell	23	F
Andrea	25	F	Ansley	22	M	Archelaus	34	M
Andreanna	36	F	Anson	18	M	Archer	35	M
Andreas	26	M	Anstice	26	M	Archibald	40	M
Andree	29	F	Anston	20	M	Archimedes	49	M
Andrei	33	M	Antaine	28	M	Ardelle	30	F
Andres	25	M	Antal	12	M	Arden	24	M
Andrew	29	M	Ante	13	M	Ardley	29	M
Andria	29	F	Anthea	22	F	Ardolph	29	M
Andriessen	45	M	Anthony	34	M	Arend	24	M
Androcles	37	M	Antigone	40	F	Areta	18	F
Andromeda	39	F	Antinous	32	M	Aretas	19	M
Andronicus	46	M	Antoine	33	M	Aretha	26	F
Ane	11	F	Antoinette	42	F	Argus	21	M
Aneira	30	F	Anton	19	M	Argyle	32	M
Aneurin	37	M	Antonella	31	F	Ari	19	B
Angel	21	M	Antonetta	29	F	Aria	20	F
Angela	22	F	Antoni	28	M	Ariadne	34	F
Angele	26	F	Antonia	29	F	Arialh	31	F
Angelica	34	F	Antonica	32	F	Ariana	26	F
Angelo	27	M	Antonina	34	F	Ariane	30	F
Angharad	36	M	Antonio	34	M	Ariel	27	B
Angus	17	M	Antons	20	M	Ariella	31	F
Angwyn	30	M	Antony	26	M	Arielle	35	F
Anica	19	F	Antonya	27	F	Arien	29	M
Aniela	24	F	Anwell	22	M	Arika	31	F
Anika	27	F	Anwyl	21	M	Ariki	39	M
Anita	18	F	Anya	14	F	Arisa	21	F
Ann	11	F	Anyon	24	M	Arisai	30	M
Anna	12	F	Anzley	29	F	Aristides	41	M
Annabel	22	F	Aodh	19	M	Aristo	28	M
Annabella	26	F	Aophonse	39	M	Aristocles	40	M
Annabelle	30	F	Aphrodite	51	F	Aristole	36	M
Annali	24	F	Apoline	36	F	Aristotle	38	M
Annan	17	M	Apollo	26	M	Arlen	23	M
Anne	16	F	Apollonia	41	F	Arlene	28	F
Annelise	34	F	April	29	F	Arlington	47	M
Annetta	21	F	Aquila	25	B	Armand	24	M
Annette	25	F	Arabela	22	F	Armando	30	M
Annica	24	F	Arabella	25	F	Armide	32	F
Annie	25	F	Arabelle	29	F	Armon	25	M
Annika	32	F	Arafat	20	M	Armorel	37	F
Annis	21	F	Aralt	16	M	Arnaldo	29	M
Anno	17	M	Araluen	27	M	Arnall	22	M
Annora	27	F	Aram	15	M	Arne	20	M
Annunciata	35	F	Aran	16	M	Arno	21	M
Ansel	15	M	Arana	17	M	Arnold	28	M
Ansell	18	M	Arbel	20	F	Arnoldine	47	F

Arod	20	M	Astrophel	42	M	Austonia	28	F
Arold	23	M	Athanasius	32	M	Autumn	18	F
Aron	21	M	Athela	20	F	Ava	24	F
Arora	26	F	Athena	22	F	Avalon	38	F
Arrian	34	M	Atherton	38	M	Avan	29	M
Artemas	23	M	Atho	17	M	Avara	34	F
Arthfael	35	M	Athol	20	M	Avel	31	M
Arthur	32	M	Ativee	44	M	Aveline	50	F
Artina	27	F	Atlanta	15	F	Avenall	40	M
Artur	24	M	Attila	18	M	Avenida	47	F
Arturo	30	M	Attracta	21	F	Averell	48	M
Arundel	30	M	Auberon	31	M	Averil	49	B
Arva	33	F	Aubin	20	M	Avery	44	M
Arvad	37	M	Aubrey	27	M	Avir	41	M
Arval	36	M	Auburn	23	M	Aviv	54	M
Arvin	46	M	Audley	23	M	Aviva	55	F
Arvis	42	M	Audre	22	F	Avoca	33	F
Asa	3	B	Audree	27	F	Avon	34	M
Asaph	18	M	Audrey	29	F	Avram	37	M
Ascelin	27	M	Audric	29	M	Avril	44	F
Ascot	13	M	Audrie	31	F	Axel	15	M
Asella	14	F	Audrye	29	F	Avfara	25	F
Ash	10	M	Audwin	27	M	Ayla	12	F
Asha	11	F	August	17	B	Aylee	21	F
Ashburn	29	M	Augusta	18	F	Ayleen	26	F
Ashburton	37	M	Auguste	22	M	Aylie	25	F
Ashby	19	M	Augustinas	33	M	Aylmer	29	M
Asher	24	M	Augustine	36	M	Aylssa	14	F
Ashford	35	M	Augustino	37	M	Aylwen	26	F
Ashlea	19	F	Augustus	21	M	Aymon	23	M
Ashlee	23	F	Aulay	15	M	Ayward	27	M
Ashleigh	42	B	Aura	14	F	Azalea	19	F
Ashley	25	B	Aurea	19	F	Azaliah	31	F
Ashlin	27	M	Aurel	21	M	Azaria	29	F
Ashton	23	M	Aurelia	31	F	Azariah	37	F
Ashur	22	M	Aurelie	35	F	Azarias	30	M
Aspasia	21	F	Aurelio	36	M	Azelia	27	F
Assar	13	M	Aurelius	34	M	Aziza	27	F
Assumption	39	F	Aurella	31	F	Azora	25	F
Assunta	14	F	Auriol	31	F	Azriel	35	M
Asta	5	F	Aurnia	28	F	Azzo	23	M
Astarte	21	F	Aurora	29	F	Baba	6	F
Aster	18	F	Aurore	33	F	Babette	19	F
Asteria	28	F	Auryn	25	M	Babilla	21	F
Aston	15	M	Austell	18	M	Babs	6	F
Astra	14	F	Austen	17	M	Baden	17	M
Astrid	26	F	Austin	21	M	Baez	16	M
Astride	31	F	Austina	22	F	Bahadur	28	M

Bailey	27	B	Barnard	31	M	Becan	16	M
Bailintin	45	M	Barnet	24	M	Beckie	35	F
Bainbridge	53	M	Barnett	26	M	Becky	28	F
Baird	25	M	Barney	29	M	Bede	16	M
Baker	28	M	Barnum	24	M	Bedelia	29	F
Bal	6	M	Baron	23	M	Bedivere	61	F
Bala	7	M	Barr	21	M	Bee	12	F
Balbina	23	F	Barret	28	M	Begga	22	F
Balbo	14	M	Barrett	30	M	Bela	11	M
Balder	24	M	Barrie	35	B	Belda	15	F
Baldred	28	M	Barris	31	M	Beldon	25	M
Baldwin	29	M	Barron	32	M	Beli	19	M
Balfour	30	M	Barry	28	B	Belica	23	F
Balin	20	M	Bart	14	M	Belina	25	F
Ballina	24	M	Bartholomew	51	M	Belinda	29	F
Balthasar	28	M	Bartley	29	M	Bella	14	F
Balunn	19	M	Barton	25	M	Bellamy	25	M
Bambalina	28	F	Bartram	28	M	Belle	18	F
Bambi	18	F	Baruch	26	M	Bellinda	32	F
Bancroft	34	M	Barwon	28	M	Belva	33	F
Bannerjee	38	M	Basia	14	F	Ben	12	M
Banning	34	M	Basil	16	M	Bendis	26	F
Banquo	25	M	Basile	21	M	Benedetta	31	F
Bapp	17	M	Basilia	26	F	Benedetto	36	M
Baptist	24	M	Basillia	29	F	Benedict	35	M
Baptista	25	F	Bassa	6	F	Benedicta	36	F
Baptisto	30	M	Bathsheba	30	F	Benedictina	50	F
Bara	13	F	Baum	10	M	Benedicto	41	M
Baraba	16	M	Baume	15	M	Benen	22	M
Baradine	36	M	Baxter	25	M	Benhur	32	M
Barak	24	M	Bayard	24	M	Beniah	30	M
Barba	15	F	Bazel	19	M	Benilda	29	F
Barbara	25	F	Bazza	20	M	Benita	24	F
Barbea	20	F	Bea	8	F	Benite	28	F
Barbery	35	M	Beagan	21	M	Benito	29	M
Barbie	28	F	Beal	11	M	Benjamin	32	M
Barbra	24	F	Beathan	24	M	Bennelong	43	M
Barclay	26	M	Beatrice	36	F	Bennett	26	M
Barden	26	M	Beatriks	40	F	Beno	18	M
Bardick	39	M	Beatrix	34	F	Benoit	29	M
Bardin	30	M	Beatriz	36	F	Benoni	32	M
Bardinga	38	M	Beattie	26	M	Benson	24	M
Bardo	22	M	Beau	11	M	Bentley	29	M
Bardolf	31	M	Beaufort	34	M	Bento	20	M
Barica	25	F	Beaumont	28	M	Benton	25	B
Barlow	26	M	Beauregard	46	M	Benvenura	57	F
Barnabas	22	M	Beauvais	44	M	Benzel	28	M
Barnaby	27	M	Bebe	14	F	Bepin	28	M

Name	No.	Sex	Name	No.	Sex	Name	No.	Sex
Beppi	30	M	Beth	17	F	Birin	34	M
Beppo	27	M	Betha	18	F	Birley	35	M
Bercan	25	M	Bethan	23	F	Birney	37	M
Bered	25	M	Bethany	30	F	Birra	30	F
Berend	30	M	Bethel	25	F	Biruni	37	M
Berenger	47	M	Bethesda	28	F	Birwain	40	M
Berenice	43	F	Bethlem	29	M	Bjorg	25	F
Beresford	47	M	Betsy	17	F	Bjorn	23	M
Berg	23	M	Bettina	26	F	Blade	15	M
Berge	28	F	Betty	18	F	Blain	20	M
Bergen	33	M	Beulah	22	F	Blaine	25	M
Berghetta	41	F	Bevan	35	M	Blair	24	B
Berkeley	47	M	Beverlee	56	F	Blaise	21	M
Berlinda	38	F	Beverleigh	75	F	Blake	22	M
Bermilla	36	F	Beverley	58	F	Blanca	15	F
Bern	21	M	Beverlie	60	F	Blanche	27	F
Bernabe	29	M	Beverly	53	M	Blanka	23	F
Bernadette	40	F	Bevin	43	F	Blase	12	M
Bernadine	45	F	Bevis	39	M	Blaxland	25	M
Bernal	25	M	Beynon	30	M	Blaze	19	M
Bernard	35	M	Bhagavati	53	F	Blenda	20	M
Bernarda	36	F	Bhaltair	35	M	Bligh	29	M
Bernardo	41	M	Bhama	16	M	Bliss	16	B
Berneen	36	F	Bhima	24	M	Blossom	23	F
Berngard	42	M	Biagio	34	M	Blue	13	M
Bernhart	41	M	Bianca	21	F	Bluesky	32	F
Bernia	31	F	Bibi	22	F	Blumenthal	36	M
Bernice	38	F	Bibiana	29	F	Blyth	22	M
Bernstein	43	M	Bice	19	F	Blythe	27	B
Berrigan	47	M	Bickel	33	M	Bnar	17	M
Berrilee	47	F	Biddy	26	F	Boaz	17	M
Berringar	56	M	Bijan	18	F	Bob	10	M
Berrookborn	76	M	Bijou	21	F	Bobak	22	M
Berry	32	B	Bika	23	F	Bobbie	26	F
Bert	18	M	Bilhilda	39	F	Bobby	19	B
Berta	19	F	Bill	17	M	Boden	22	M
Bertha	27	F	Billa	18	F	Bodil	24	F
Berthe	31	F	Billee	27	F	Bogart	27	M
Berthold	39	M	Billie	31	F	Boguslaw	28	M
Bertilia	40	F	Billy	24	M	Boleslav	43	M
Bertilla	34	F	Biloela	29	M	Bonamy	25	M
Bertram	32	M	Bilyana	28	M	Bonar	23	M
Bertrand	37	M	Bilyarra	41	M	Bondi	26	F
Berwyn	33	F	Bina	17	F	Boniface	37	M
Beryl	26	F	Bing	23	M	Bonita	25	F
Bess	9	F	Bird	24	F	Bonne	23	F
Bessie	23	F	Birdie	38	F	Bonnie	32	F
Beta	10	F	Birget	34	F	Bonny	25	F

Bono	19	M	Branwell	33	M	Bromwen	36	F
Bonosa	21	F	Branwen	32	F	Bron	22	M
Boolee	27	M	Bray	19	M	Brona	23	F
Boondoon	40	M	Brazil	32	M	Bronson	34	M
Booral	27	M	Brecon	30	M	Bronte	29	F
Booran	29	M	Bree	21	F	Bronwen	37	F
Booreah	37	M	Breese	27	M	Bronwyn	39	F
Booth	24	M	Brenda	26	F	Bronya	30	F
Bootoolga	39	M	Brendan	31	M	Brook	34	F
Borden	31	M	Brendon	36	M	Brooke	39	F
Boreen	32	M	Brenna	27	F	Brough	35	M
Borg	24	M	Brent	23	M	Broughton	48	M
Boris	27	M	Brenton	34	M	Bruce	22	M
Boronia	38	F	Bret	18	M	Bruin	28	M
Boswell	25	M	Brett	20	M	Bruna	20	F
Bosworth	39	M	Briallen	37	F	Brunella	31	F
Bowen	23	M	Brian	26	M	Brunetta	29	F
Bowie	27	M	Briana	27	F	Brunhilda	44	F
Bowral	26	F	Brianna	32	F	Bruno	25	M
Bowyer	34	M	Brianne	36	F	Brunton	32	M
Boyce	23	M	Briar	30	F	Bryan	24	M
Boyd	19	M	Brice	28	M	Bryce	26	M
Boyden	29	M	Bride	29	F	Brychan	35	M
Boyle	23	M	Bridey	36	F	Bryde	27	F
Boynton	33	M	Bridget	38	F	Brydie	36	F
Bozidar	39	M	Bridgid	44	F	Bryna	24	F
Bozo	22	M	Brie	25	F	Brynhild	47	F
Brad	16	M	Brien	30	M	Brynn	28	M
Bradburn	35	M	Brighid	48	F	Bryony	36	F
Braden	26	M	Brigid	40	F	Buadhach	30	M
Bradford	41	M	Brigida	41	F	Bud	9	M
Bradley	31	M	Brigitte	45	F	Budd	13	M
Bradman	26	M	Bringham	45	M	Buddy	20	M
Bradwell	32	M	Brinley	40	M	Budgeree	40	M
Brady	23	M	Brinsley	41	M	Buena	16	F
Brae	17	B	Brionie	45	F	Bulooral	33	M
Bram	16	M	Briony	38	F	Bunty	19	F
Bramwell	32	M	Brita	23	F	Burden	28	M
Bran	17	M	Britannia	43	F	Burdon	29	M
Branca	21	F	Brites	28	F	Burgess	28	M
Branch	28	F	Britney	39	F	Burgh	29	M
Brand	21	M	Britt	24	F	Buri	23	M
Brandan	27	M	Brittany	37	F	Burke	30	M
Brandi	30	F	Brock	31	M	Burl	17	M
Brandon	32	M	Brockwell	47	M	Burleigh	46	M
Brandy	28	F	Broderick	58	M	Burley	29	M
Branko	34	M	Brodie	35	M	Burne	24	M
Brant	19	M	Brody	28	M	Burnell	30	M

Burnell	30	M	Calca	11	F	Carey	25	B
Burnett	28	M	Calder	25	M	Cari	22	F
Burnetta	29	F	Caldwell	27	M	Carice	30	F
Burns	20	M	Cale	12	M	Carilla	29	F
Burnum	26	M	Caleb	14	M	Carin	27	F
Burr	23	M	Caley	19	M	Carina	28	F
Burt	16	M	Calhoun	29	M	Carine	32	F
Burton	27	M	Cali	16	F	Carinthia	47	F
Butch	18	M	Calida	21	F	Carisa	24	F
Butler	24	M	Calista	20	F	Carissa	25	F
Buto	13	F	Calisto	25	M	Carita	25	F
Buttercup	36	F	Calla	11	F	Carl	16	M
Byblis	24	F	Callaghan	32	M	Carla	17	F
Byng	21	M	Callagun	26	M	Carleen	31	F
Byram	23	M	Callan	16	M	Carleton	34	M
Byrger	39	M	Calleen	25	F	Carlin	30	M
Byrne	28	M	Callista	23	F	Carlina	31	F
Byron	29	M	Callula	17	F	Carline	35	F
Cabarita	28	F	Callum	17	M	Carlisle	34	M
Cacre	21	M	Calphurnia	49	F	Carlo	22	M
Cadbury	29	M	Calpurnia	41	F	Carlos	23	M
Caddie	26	F	Calvin	43	M	Carlota	25	F
Caddy	19	F	Calypso	28	F	Carlotta	27	F
Cadel	16	M	Camden	22	M	Carlton	29	M
Cadell	19	M	Camelia	26	F	Carly	23	F
Cadence	26	F	Camellia	29	F	Carlyle	31	M
Cadenza	27	F	Cameo	19	F	Carma	18	F
Cadeyrn	34	M	Cameron	33	M	Carmel	25	F
Cadfael	23	M	Camila	21	F	Carmela	26	F
Cadfan	20	M	Camilla	24	F	Carmelita	37	F
Cadifor	38	M	Camille	28	F	Carmen	27	F
Cadiz	25	M	Camillo	29	M	Carmenta	30	F
Cadman	18	F	Camira	27	F	Carmichael	46	M
Cadmus	16	M	Campbell	28	M	Carmine	36	F
Cadwell	24	M	Canberra	35	F	Carnation	41	F
Caera	19	F	Candace	22	F	Carney	30	M
Caesar	20	M	Candice	30	F	Carol	22	B
Caesaria	30	F	Candido	32	M	Carole	27	F
Cahil	24	M	Cane	14	M	Carolina	37	F
Cahill	27	M	Capri	29	F	Caroline	41	F
Cahn	17	M	Caprice	37	F	Carolyn	34	F
Cailean	27	M	Capucine	36	F	Caronwen	39	F
Cain	18	M	Cara	14	F	Carr	22	M
Cairene	37	F	Caragh	29	F	Carrick	45	M
Cairine	41	F	Caralyn	29	F	Carrie	36	F
Caitlyn	30	F	Cardinia	41	F	Carroll	34	B
Calandra	27	F	Caren	23	F	Carryl	32	F
Calantha	24	F	Carenne	33	F	Carson	25	M

Carter	29	M	Celandine	40	F	Charleene	44	F
Cartin	29	F	Celena	22	F	Charles	30	M
Carver	49	M	Celene	26	F	Charley	36	F
Cary	20	M	Celesta	20	F	Charlie	38	M
Caryl	23	F	Celeste	24	F	Charline	43	F
Casandra	25	F	Celestino	39	M	Charlotte	39	F
Casey	17	B	Celia	21	F	Charlton	37	M
Casilda	22	F	Celie	25	F	Charmaine	45	F
Casimir	36	M	Celine	30	F	Charmian	40	F
Casimira	37	F	Cellandine	43	F	Charo	27	F
Caspar	22	M	Celosia	28	F	Chase	18	M
Caspara	23	F	Celynen	33	M	Chastity	33	F
Cassandra	26	F	Cera	18	F	Chauncey	35	M
Cassel	14	M	Cerelia	35	F	Chava	35	F
Cassem	15	M	Ceres	23	F	Cheiro	40	M
Cassia	16	F	Ceri	26	M	Cheiron	45	M
Cassidy	26	M	Cerian	32	F	Chelcie	36	F
Cassie	20	F	Ceridwen	45	F	Chelsea	26	F
Cassius	19	M	Cerilia	39	F	Chemarin	44	F
Castor	22	M	Cerise	32	F	Chemosh	35	F
Catalina	25	F	Cerwyn	34	M	Chen	21	M
Catana	13	F	Cerys	25	F	Cheney	33	M
Catarina	31	F	Cesar	19	M	Cheng	28	M
Cate	11	F	Cesca	13	F	Cher	25	F
Caterina	35	F	Cesilia	31	F	Chera	26	F
Catharina	39	F	Chad	16	M	Cheri	34	F
Catherine	47	F	Chadwick	44	M	Cherie	39	F
Cathleen	32	F	Chaim	25	M	Cherilyn	49	F
Cathmor	33	M	Chalice	32	F	Cherise	40	F
Catlin	23	F	Chalmer	33	M	Cherry	41	F
Cato	12	M	Chan	17	M	Cheryl	35	F
Caton	17	M	Chandler	38	M	Chesney	34	M
Catrice	32	F	Chandra	31	B	Chester	33	M
Catrine	34	F	Chanel	25	F	Chevy	45	M
Catriona	36	F	Chang	24	M	Cheyenne	43	M
Cavan	32	M	Chantal	23	F	Chiang	33	M
Cavell	37	M	Chantel	27	F	Chiara	31	F
Cavill	41	M	Chantelle	35	F	Chico	29	M
Cawley	24	M	Chapin	33	M	Chilla	27	M
Cecil	23	M	Chapman	29	M	Chilton	36	M
Cecile	28	F	Chara	22	F	Chin	25	M
Cecilia	33	F	Charis	31	F	Chiquita	43	F
Cecilie	37	F	Charisma	36	F	Chitty	31	M
Cecily	30	F	Charissa	33	F	Chloe	25	F
Cecilya	31	F	Charita	33	F	Chloris	39	F
Cedric	33	M	Charitina	47	F	Chou	20	M
Ceinlys	33	F	Charity	39	F	Chris	30	B
Ceinwen	37	F	Charleen	39	F	Chriselda	43	F

Christa	33	F	Clairmond	44	F	Clio	21	F
Christabel	43	F	Clan	12	M	Clive	42	M
Christabelle	51	F	Clancy	22	M	Cloe	17	F
Christal	36	F	Clara	17	F	Clorinda	40	F
Christanta	41	F	Clarabelle	35	F	Cloris	31	F
Christel	40	F	Clare	21	F	Clorita	33	F
Christian	47	M	Clarence	34	B	Clova	35	F
Christiane	52	F	Claresta	25	F	Clover	48	F
Christianna	53	F	Claribel	35	F	Clovis	44	M
Christie	46	F	Clarice	33	F	Cluny	21	F
Christina	47	F	Clarinda	35	F	Clydai	27	M
Christine	51	F	Clarissa	28	F	Clyde	22	M
Christinha	55	F	Clarisse	32	F	Clydia	27	F
Christmas	38	F	Clarita	28	F	Clymene	32	F
Christobel	48	F	Clark	27	M	Clythe	28	F
Christobella	52	F	Clarke	32	M	Clytie	29	F
Christofer	58	M	Claud	14	M	Coba	12	F
Christoffer	64	M	Claude	19	M	Cocha	21	F
Christopher	67	M	Claudette	28	F	Coco	18	F
Christophera	68	F	Claudia	24	F	Codey	25	M
Christopherine	86	F	Claudina	29	F	Coel	17	M
Christos	39	M	Claudine	33	F	Coen	19	M
Chrysander	52	M	Claudio	29	M	Coffey	33	M
Chrystal	34	F	Claus	11	M	Cohen	27	M
Chu	14	B	Clavier	52	F	Col	12	M
Chuca	18	F	Clay	14	M	Cola	13	M
Chuchita	37	F	Clayton	27	M	Colba	15	F
Chueh	27	M	Cle	11	F	Colby	21	M
Cian	18	F	Clea	12	F	Cole	17	M
Ciar	22	F	Cleantha	28	F	Coleman	27	M
Cicely	30	F	Cleary	28	M	Coletta	22	F
Cicero	35	M	Cledwyn	32	M	Colette	26	F
Cid	16	M	Clematis	28	F	Colgan	25	M
Cien	22	M	Clemence	33	F	Colin	26	M
Cilla	19	F	Clemency	35	F	Colina	27	F
Cindi	30	F	Clement	27	M	Colinette	40	F
Cindie	35	F	Clemente	32	B	Colleen	30	F
Cindy	28	F	Clementia	37	F	Colley	27	M
Cindylou	40	F	Clementine	46	F	Collin	29	M
Cinnamon	38	F	Cleo	17	F	Columbia	31	B
Cinnia	32	F	Cleon	22	M	Columbina	36	F
Ciorsdan	38	F	Cleopatra	37	F	Columbine	40	F
Ciril	33	M	Cliantha	32	F	Combara	26	F
Cirilla	37	F	Cliff	27	M	Comfort	36	F
Cirilo	39	M	Clifford	46	M	Compton	33	M
Cissie	28	F	Clifton	34	M	Comyn	25	M
Clair	25	F	Clint	22	M	Con	14	M
Claire	30	F	Clinton	33	M	Conal	18	M

Conan	20	M	Corinne	42	F	Cromwell	38	M
Concepcion	52	F	Coriss	29	F	Crosbie	35	B
Conception	51	F	Corissa	30	F	Crosby	28	M
Concetta	27	F	Corliss	32	F	Crystal	26	F
Concha	26	F	Cormac	26	M	Cuc	9	F
Conchita	37	F	Cornelia	41	F	Cullen	22	M
Conchubhar	48	M	Cornelie	45	F	Culley	24	M
Concordia	46	F	Cornelio	46	M	Culver	45	M
Confucius	39	M	Cornelis	41	M	Cuong	24	M
Cong	21	M	Cornelius	44	M	Curra	25	F
Coniah	32	M	Cornish	41	M	Curran	30	M
Conlan	23	M	Corona	30	F	Curringa	46	M
Conn	19	M	Corra	28	F	Currita	36	F
Connie	33	F	Cort	20	M	Curt	17	M
Connor	34	M	Cory	25	M	Curtis	27	M
Conor	29	F	Corydon	40	M	Cushla	19	F
Conrad	28	M	Cosette	24	F	Custance	23	F
Conradine	47	F	Cosima	24	F	Cuthbert	34	M
Conroy	36	M	Cosimo	29	M	Cuthberta	35	F
Consolata	28	F	Cosmas	16	M	Cutler	25	M
Constance	31	F	Cosmo	20	M	Cybele	25	F
Constancia	36	F	Courtenay	41	B	Cybil	24	F
Constancio	41	M	Courtney	40	B	Cybill	27	F
Constant	25	M	Coventry	59	M	Cynara	26	F
Constantia	35	F	Covey	43	M	Cyndeyrn	45	M
Constantin	39	M	Cowan	20	M	Cyndi	28	F
Constantina	40	F	Cradock	37	M	Cynfael	30	M
Constantine	44	M	Craig	29	M	Cynfor	36	M
Constitucion	54	M	Crandall	29	M	Cyngen	32	M
Consuela	27	F	Crandell	33	M	Cynthia	35	F
Consuelo	32	F	Cranog	31	M	Cyprian	41	M
Content	28	F	Crawford	43	M	Cypriana	42	F
Conway	27	M	Creighton	54	M	Cyr	19	M
Cooba	18	M	Crescent	33	F	Cyra	20	F
Coolalie	36	F	Cressida	33	F	Cyrano	31	M
Cora	19	F	Cresswell	35	M	Cyrena	30	F
Coral	22	F	Crighton	49	M	Cyria	29	F
Coralice	39	F	Crisiant	39	F	Cyril	31	M
Coralie	36	F	Crispian	44	M	Cyrilla	35	F
Corazon	38	F	Crispin	43	M	Cyrille	39	F
Corbin	34	M	Crispina	44	F	Cyrus	23	M
Cordelia	40	F	Cristal	28	F	Cyryl	29	M
Cordell	33	M	Cristian	39	M	Cythera	35	F
Cordella	34	F	Cristina	39	F	Cytherea	40	F
Corel	26	F	Cristobal	36	M	Czenzi	38	F
Coretta	28	F	Cristy	31	F	Dacey	20	M
Corey	30	M	Crocus	25	F	Dacia	18	F
Corinna	38	F	Crofton	37	M	Daffodil	39	F

Name	Value	Sex	Name	Value	Sex	Name	Value	Sex
Dag	12	M	Daniella	31	F	Dawn	15	F
Dagan	18	M	Danielle	35	F	Daya	13	F
Dagda	17	M	Danil	22	M	Dayle	20	F
Dagmar	26	F	Danila	23	F	Dayn	17	M
Dagmara	27	F	Dannel	23	M	Dea	10	M
Dagny	24	F	Danny	22	M	Dean	15	M
Dago	18	M	Dante	17	M	Deana	16	F
Dagon	23	M	Danuta	16	F	Deane	20	M
Dagwood	33	M	Daphna	26	F	Deanna	21	F
Daha	14	F	Daphne	30	F	Deanne	25	F
Dahlia	26	F	Dara	15	F	Deb	11	F
Dahna	19	F	Darata	18	F	Debbie	27	F
Dai	14	M	Darby	23	M	Debby	20	F
Daireen	38	F	Darcie	31	F	Debi	20	F
Daisy	22	F	Darcy	24	B	Debor	26	F
Dakini	39	F	Darel	22	F	Deborah	35	F
Dalasaid	25	F	Darerca	32	F	Debra	21	F
Dale	13	B	Dargan	27	M	Deda	14	F
Dalenna	24	F	Daria	24	F	Dee	14	F
Dalia	18	F	Darianne	39	F	Defail	28	M
Dallan	17	M	Darice	31	F	Dei	18	F
Dallas	13	B	Darien	33	M	Deidre	36	F
Dalman	18	M	Darius	27	M	Deirdre	45	F
Dalton	21	M	Darleen	32	F	Delano	24	M
Daltrey	31	M	Darlene	32	F	Delbert	30	M
Dalziel	33	M	Darline	36	F	Delcine	34	F
Damalis	23	F	Darnell	30	M	Delfina	33	F
Damaris	29	F	Daron	25	F	Delfine	37	F
Damian	24	M	Darran	29	M	Delia	22	F
Damiana	25	F	Darrell	34	M	Delice	29	F
Damien	28	M	Darren	33	M	Delicia	34	F
Damita	21	F	Darrin	37	M	Delight	38	F
Damon	20	M	Darryl	33	M	Delilah	33	F
Damosel	24	F	Darton	27	M	Delinda	31	F
Damsel	18	F	Darwin	33	M	Delko	29	M
Damzel	25	F	Darya	22	F	Della	16	F
Dan	10	M	Daryl	24	M	Delma	17	F
Dana	11	B	Daryll	27	F	Delmar	26	M
Danae	16	F	Dat	7	M	Delora	28	F
Dancel	21	M	Dauntie	29	F	Delores	33	F
Dane	15	M	Davey	39	M	Delphine	46	F
Danella	22	F	David	40	M	Delta	15	F
Danetta	20	F	Davida	41	F	Delvene	49	F
Danette	24	F	Davin	41	M	Delvin	48	F
Danica	23	F	Davina	42	F	Delvine	53	F
Daniel	27	M	Davis	37	M	Delwen	27	F
Daniela	28	F	Davita	39	F	Delwyn	29	M
Daniele	32	F	Dawed	19	M	Delyth	29	F

Demas	15	M	Devin	45	M	Divis	45	M
Demetria	39	F	Devnet	43	F	Dix	19	M
Demetrios	45	M	Devota	40	F	Dixi	33	F
Demetrius	42	M	Dewey	26	M	Dixiebelle	51	F
Demi	22	F	Dewi	23	M	Doane	21	M
Democritus	46	M	Dexter	31	M	Dobbs	15	M
Demos	20	M	Dhatri	33	M	Dobson	24	M
Dempster	37	M	Diamonda	34	F	Docilla	29	F
Dena	15	F	Diana	20	F	Dolfine	38	F
Denby	23	M	Diane	24	F	Dolly	23	F
Denham	27	M	Dianna	25	F	Dolores	34	F
Denholm	35	M	Dianne	29	F	Dolorita	40	F
Denice	31	F	Diantha	30	F	Domela	23	F
Denis	24	M	Dibble	25	M	Domenic	36	M
Denisa	25	F	Dibbs	18	M	Domenica	37	F
Denise	29	F	Dibri	33	M	Domina	29	F
Denman	24	M	Dick	27	M	Domingo	41	M
Dennis	29	M	Didier	40	M	Dominic	40	M
Denys	22	M	Diedrik	51	M	Dominica	41	F
Denzil	34	M	Diego	31	M	Dominique	53	B
Deodatus	26	M	Dietbold	35	M	Donahue	32	M
Derain	33	M	Dietbrand	41	M	Donal	19	M
Derek	34	M	Dieter	34	M	Donald	23	M
Derik	38	M	Dietman	30	M	Donalda	24	F
Derina	33	F	Dietrich	49	M	Donalta	22	F
Dermot	30	M	Digby	29	M	Donan	21	M
Dermott	32	M	Digger	41	M	Donata	19	F
Derren	37	M	Dillon	30	M	Donatello	35	M
Derrick	50	M	Dilys	24	F	Donato	24	M
Derrin	41	M	Dimiter	42	M	Donatus	22	M
Derry	34	M	Dimitiris	56	M	Donegal	31	M
Derryn	39	B	Dimitra	38	F	Donella	27	F
Derryth	44	F	Dimity	35	F	Donia	25	F
Dervla	44	F	Dina	19	F	Donna	21	F
Derward	37	M	Dinah	27	F	Donnan	26	M
Derwen	33	F	Dinewan	34	M	Donoghue	44	M
Derwent	35	M	Dinna	24	F	Donovan	49	M
Derwin	37	M	Dino	24	M	Doongara	39	M
Derwyn	35	F	Dinsdale	32	M	Dora	20	F
Desdemona	35	F	Diocles	31	M	Dorak	31	M
Desiree	38	F	Diomede	37	M	Doralia	33	F
Desley	25	F	Dion	24	B	Doralicia	45	F
Desma	15	F	Dione	29	F	Doran	25	M
Desmona	26	F	Dionetta	34	F	Dorcas	24	B
Desmond	29	M	Dionne	34	F	Dore	24	B
Deva	32	F	Dionnetta	39	F	Doree	29	F
Devaki	52	F	Dionysius	45	M	Doreen	34	F
Devi	40	F	Dirk	33	M	Doretta	29	F

Dorette	33	F	Dunstan	21	M	Eden	19	F
Doria	29	F	Dura	17	F	Edgar	26	M
Dorian	34	M	Dural	20	M	Edie	23	F
Dorice	36	F	Duran	22	M	Edin	23	M
Dorien	38	M	Durand	26	M	Edina	24	F
Dorinda	38	F	Durant	24	M	Edison	30	M
Doris	29	F	Durrebar	42	M	Edith	28	F
Dorita	31	F	Durward	35	M	Edmond	28	M
Doron	30	M	Dusa	9	F	Edmonda	29	F
Dorotea	33	F	Dusan	14	M	Edmondo	34	M
Dorothea	41	F	Duscha	20	F	Edmonton	37	F
Dorothee	45	F	Dustin	24	M	Edmund	25	M
Dorothy	42	F	Dusty	17	F	Edna	15	F
Dorrie	42	F	Dwayne	27	M	Edon	20	F
Dorryn	40	M	Dwight	35	M	Edra	19	F
Dory	26	M	Dyan	17	F	Edric	30	M
Dougal	24	M	Dyfan	23	M	Edris	28	F
Douglas	25	M	Dylan	20	M	Edryd	29	M
Douglass	26	F	Dymock	35	M	Edsel	18	M
Douna	19	F	Dyna	17	F	Edson	21	M
Dove	37	F	Dynawd	26	M	Eduard	26	M
Dover	46	M	Dysis	22	F	Eduardo	32	M
Doyle	25	M	Eachan	23	M	Edwald	22	M
Dragan	27	M	Eachunn	30	M	Edward	28	M
Drake	30	M	Eadgar	27	M	Edwardine	47	F
Drenka	35	F	Eamon	21	M	Edwin	28	M
Drew	23	M	Eanruig	39	M	Edwina	29	F
Drina	28	F	Earl	18	M	Edwy	21	M
Driscoll	38	M	Earle	23	M	Effie	31	F
Drostan	28	M	Earnest	28	M	Efram	25	M
Dru	16	M	Eartha	26	F	Egan	18	M
Druce	24	M	Easter	23	F	Egbert	30	M
Druella	28	F	Ebba	10	F	Egerton	39	M
Drummond	39	M	Eben	17	M	Egide	30	M
Drusilla	33	F	Ebenezer	44	M	Egidion	45	M
Drystan	29	M	Eber	21	M	Egidius	38	M
Duana	14	F	Ebert	23	M	Eglah	24	F
Duane	18	M	Eberta	24	F	Egmont	29	M
Duarte	24	M	Ebony	25	F	Egon	23	M
Dudley	26	M	Eckart	31	M	Egor	27	M
Duff	19	M	Eckhardt	43	M	Ehren	32	M
Dugald	22	M	Eda	10	F	Ehud	20	M
Dugan	20	M	Edan	15	M	Eileen	32	F
Duke	23	M	Edana	16	F	Eilene	32	F
Dula	11	F	Edbert	27	M	Eilis	27	F
Dulcie	27	F	Eddie	27	M	Eilwen	32	F
Duncan	21	M	Edeline	36	F	Einar	29	M
Dunmore	36	M	Edelyn	29	F	Einfeld	37	M

Eira	24	F	Elian	23	M	Elrica	30	F
Eirian	38	F	Elias	19	M	Elridge	42	M
Eiric	35	F	Elidr	30	M	Elroy	30	M
Eirig	39	M	Eliezer	44	M	Elsa	10	F
Eirik	43	M	Elihu	28	M	Else	14	F
Eiros	30	M	Elijah	27	M	Elsie	23	F
Eirwen	38	F	Elined	31	F	Elspeth	31	F
Eisenbart	39	M	Eliot	25	M	Elston	22	M
Eisenbolt	38	M	Eliott	27	M	Elswyth	31	F
Eithne	34	F	Eliphalet	43	M	Elton	21	M
Ekala	21	F	Elisa	19	F	Elva	31	F
El	8	M	Elisabetta	31	F	Elvin	44	M
Elaeth	24	M	Elise	23	F	Elvina	45	F
Elaine	28	F	Elisha	27	M	Elvira	49	F
Elan	14	F	Elissa	20	F	Elvis	40	M
Elana	15	F	Elita	20	F	Elwin	27	M
Elanora	30	F	Eliza	26	F	Elwood	29	M
Elata	12	F	Elizabella	40	F	Elwy	20	F
Elberta	27	F	Elizabeth	43	F	Elwyn	25	B
Eldad	17	M	Elkanah	34	M	Elyne	25	F
Elder	26	M	Ella	12	F	Elysia	26	F
Eldon	23	M	Ellamay	24	F	Ema	10	F
Eldora	28	F	Elle	16	F	Emanuel	22	M
Eldred	30	M	Ellen	21	F	Emanuela	27	F
Eldrida	35	F	Ellery	32	M	Embia	21	F
Eldwin	31	M	Elli	20	F	Embla	15	F
Eleanor	34	F	Ellice	28	F	Embrance	34	F
Eleanora	35	F	Ellie	25	F	Eme	14	F
Eleanore	39	F	Ellin	25	F	Emelda	22	F
Eleazar	32	M	Elliot	28	M	Emelia	27	F
Electra	28	F	Elliott	30	M	Emeline	36	F
Elefreda	38	F	Ellis	21	M	Emelye	29	F
Elen	18	F	Ellison	32	M	Emer	23	F
Elena	19	F	Ellsworth	42	M	Emera	24	F
Elene	23	F	Elly	18	F	Emerald	31	F
Eleni	27	F	Ellyn	23	F	Emerentia	45	F
Eleonore	44	F	Elma	13	F	Emeric	35	M
Eleutherios	56	M	Elmar	22	M	Emerson	35	M
Elfira	33	F	Elmer	26	M	Emery	30	M
Elfleda	27	F	Elmina	27	F	Emey	21	F
Elfred	32	M	Elmira	31	F	Emil	21	M
Elga	16	F	Elmo	18	M	Emile	26	M
Elgar	25	M	Elna	14	F	Emilia	31	F
Elgin	29	M	Elodie	32	F	Emiliana	37	F
Elgiva	47	F	Eloisa	25	F	Emilie	35	F
Eli	17	M	Eloise	29	F	Emilio	36	M
Elia	18	M	Elora	24	F	Emily	28	F
Eliab	20	M	Elouera	32	F	Emina	24	F

Emlyn	24	M	Erastus	22	M	Esme	15	B
Emma	14	F	Erberto	38	M	Esmeralda	33	F
Emmaline	36	F	Ercole	31	M	Esmond	25	M
Emmanuel	30	M	Eremelinda	50	F	Esperance	41	F
Emmanuela	31	F	Erhardt	36	M	Esperanza	42	F
Emmanuelle	38	F	Eric	26	M	Essie	21	F
Emmeline	40	F	Erica	27	F	Essington	41	M
Emmelyn	33	F	Erich	34	M	Essylit	28	F
Emmet	20	M	Ericha	35	F	Esta	9	F
Emmett	22	M	Erik	34	M	Estavan	37	M
Emmeric	43	M	Erika	35	F	Este	13	M
Emmon	24	M	Erin	28	B	Esteban	21	M
Emmylou	32	F	Erina	29	F	Estella	20	F
Emory	31	M	Erinn	33	F	Estelle	24	F
Emry	25	M	Erl	17	M	Ester	22	F
Emrys	26	M	Erland	27	M	Estera	23	F
Ena	11	F	Erlina	32	F	Esterre	36	F
Endor	29	M	Erline	36	F	Estevan	41	M
Endres	29	M	Erling	38	M	Esther	30	F
Eneas	17	M	Erma	19	F	Estrelita	37	F
Engel	25	F	Ermanno	35	M	Estrella	29	F
Engelbert	43	M	Ermas	20	F	Eswen	21	F
Engelberta	44	F	Ermin	32	M	Ethan	21	M
Engelina	40	F	Ermo	24	M	Ethel	23	F
Engracia	40	F	Erna	20	F	Ethell	26	F
Enid	23	F	Ernacta	26	F	Etienne	36	M
Ennion	35	F	Ernald	27	M	Etta	10	F
Ennis	25	B	Ernest	27	M	Ettie	23	F
Enoch	27	M	Ernesta	28	F	Ettore	29	M
Enodoch	37	F	Erneste	32	M	Euan	14	M
Enola	20	F	Ernestine	46	F	Eucaria	31	F
Enos	17	M	Ernesto	33	M	Euchar	29	F
Enrichetta	49	F	Ernold	32	M	Euchario	44	F
Enrico	37	M	Ernst	22	M	Euclea	20	F
Enright	45	M	Errki	43	M	Euclid	27	M
Enrika	40	F	Errol	32	M	Eudia	22	F
Enrique	44	M	Erskine	45	M	Eudo	18	M
Enriqueta	47	F	Ertha	25	F	Eudocia	31	F
Ensor	26	M	Erwin	33	M	Eudocie	35	F
Enz	18	M	Erwina	34	F	Eudora	28	F
Eos	12	F	Eryk	32	M	Eugene	30	M
Ephraim	43	M	Eryn	26	F	Eugenia	35	F
Epona	24	F	Erzebet	36	F	Eugenie	39	F
Eramus	23	M	Esara	17	F	Eugenio	40	M
Eran	20	M	Esau	10	M	Eulalia	25	F
Eranthe	35	F	Esdras	21	M	Euloowirree	65	F
Erasma	21	F	Eskaer	32	F	Eunice	30	F
Erasmus	24	M	Esko	23	M	Euphemia	42	F

Euphrasia	44	F	Fabrice	35	M	Federico	47	M
Eureka	34	B	Fabrician	45	M	Federigo	51	M
Eurfyl	33	M	Fabrienne	47	F	Fedor	30	M
Eurwen	32	F	Fabron	29	M	Fedora	31	F
Eurydice	45	F	Fadil	23	M	Felda	19	F
Eusebuis	29	M	Fagan	20	M	Felice	31	B
Eustace	20	M	Fagin	28	M	Felicia	36	F
Eustacia	25	F	Failka	31	F	Felicity	44	F
Eustella	23	F	Faina	22	F	Felipe	35	M
Eutyches	34	M	Faine	26	F	Felix	29	M
Eva	28	F	Fairfax	38	M	Felton	27	M
Evadne	42	F	Fairlee	38	F	Fen	16	M
Evan	33	M	Fairley	40	M	Fenella	28	F
Evana	34	F	Fairlie	42	F	Fengshui	44	M
Evander	51	M	Faisel	25	M	Fenlon	30	M
Evangeline	67	F	Faith	26	F	Fenton	29	M
Evangelos	55	M	Faizah	33	F	Feodor	36	M
Evanthe	48	F	Falcon	24	M	Feodosia	38	F
Evaristus	53	M	Falkner	40	M	Ferdinand	48	M
Evart	39	M	Fanchon	34	F	Ferenc	33	M
Eve	32	F	Fanny	24	F	Fergu	30	M
Eveleen	50	F	Fantine	33	F	Fergus	31	M
Evelina	50	F	Faramond	36	M	Ferguson	42	M
Eveline	54	F	Farand	26	M	Fern	25	F
Evelyn	47	F	Farid	29	M	Fernand	35	M
Everard	55	M	Farleigh	48	M	Fernanda	36	F
Everett	50	M	Farley	31	M	Fernando	41	M
Everhard	63	M	Farnell	32	M	Ferninand	49	M
Everlida	58	F	Farnley	36	M	Ferrars	40	M
Evette	41	F	Farold	29	M	Ferris	39	M
Evita	39	F	Farquhar	45	M	Ferry	36	M
Evonne	48	F	Farr	25	M	Fidel	27	M
Evva	50	F	Farrah	34	F	Fidela	28	F
Ewa	11	F	Farrar	35	M	Fielder	41	M
Ewan	16	M	Farrell	36	M	Fielding	48	M
Ewart	22	M	Farrer	39	M	Fifi	30	F
Ewe	15	F	Farry	32	M	Fifine	40	F
Ewen	20	M	Fastmund	26	M	Figaro	38	M
Eyar	22	M	Fatima	23	F	Filep	30	M
Eydis	26	M	Faustin	27	M	Filide	36	F
Eystein	34	M	Faustino	33	M	Filipe	39	M
Ezekiel	46	M	Fausto	19	M	Filippo	47	M
Ezra	23	M	Favel	37	M	Filma	23	F
Ezzat	24	F	Fawn	17	F	Finan	26	M
Fabia	19	F	Fay	14	F	Finbar	32	M
Fabian	24	M	Fayme	23	F	Finetta	30	F
Fabien	28	M	Fazio	30	M	Fingal	31	M
Fabio	24	M	Fazl	18	M	Finian	35	M

Finigan	42	M	Forrest	38	M	Fu Chung	35	M
Finlay	31	M	Forster	38	M	Fu Hai	27	M
Finley	35	M	Fortunato	40	B	Fuad	14	M
Finn	25	M	Fossetta	24	F	Fudo	19	M
Finna	26	F	Fox	18	M	Fuji	19	M
Finnian	40	M	Franc	24	M	Fulbert	30	M
Finola	30	F	Frances	30	F	Fulco	21	M
Fiona	27	F	Francesca	34	F	Fulke	28	M
Fiorello	47	M	Francesco	39	M	Fulton	25	M
Fiske	32	M	Francis	34	M	Fulvia	44	F
Fitz	25	M	Francisco	43	M	Fursey	31	M
Fitzgerald	54	M	Franco	30	M	Fushen	28	M
Fitzhugh	51	M	Francois	40	B	Fyodor	38	M
Fitzroy	47	M	Frank	32	M	Gabela	19	M
Flaherty	41	M	Frankfort	55	M	Gabin	24	M
Flann	20	M	Frankie	46	M	Gable	18	M
Flanna	21	F	Franklin	49	M	Gabor	25	M
Flannan	26	M	Franklyn	47	M	Gabriel	36	M
Flavia	42	F	Frants	24	M	Gabriela	37	F
Flavian	47	M	Franz	29	M	Gabriele	41	M
Flavio	47	M	Fraser	31	M	Gabrielle	44	F
Flavius	45	M	Fred	24	M	Gabriello	45	M
Fleet	21	M	Freda	25	F	Gaby	17	M
Fleming	39	M	Frederic	50	M	Gad	12	M
Fleta	17	F	Frederica	51	F	Gael	16	M
Fletch	27	M	Frederick	61	M	Gaetano	27	M
Fletcher	41	M	Frederico	56	M	Gage	20	M
Fleur	26	F	Frederik	58	M	Gail	20	F
Fleurdelice	55	F	Fredson	36	M	Gair	26	M
Flinders	42	F	Freedom	39	M	Galahad	25	M
Flinn	28	M	Freeman	35	M	Galatea	20	F
Flint	25	M	Freemantle	40	M	Gale	16	B
Floero	35	M	Fremont	37	M	Galem	20	M
Flora	25	F	French	36	M	Galen	21	M
Floranthe	45	F	Frenchie	50	M	Galiena	31	F
Florence	42	F	Freya	28	F	Galilah	32	F
Florenz	42	M	Freyja	29	F	Galileo	34	M
Florian	39	M	Frick	38	M	Galina	26	F
Florimel	45	F	Fridmund	44	M	Gallagher	44	M
Florinda	43	F	Frieda	34	F	Gallipoli	48	M
Floyd	26	M	Friedmann	48	M	Galton	24	M
Flynn	26	M	Friend	38	M	Galvin	47	M
Folker	40	M	Frith	34	B	Gamal	16	M
Fonz	25	M	Fritz	34	M	Gamaliel	33	M
Fonzie	39	M	Frobisher	55	M	Gamel	20	M
Forbes	29	M	Fronde	35	F	Gamlyn	27	M
Ford	25	M	Frost	24	M	Ganan	19	M
Forest	29	M	Fu	9	M	Gandhi	34	M

Gioacchino	57	M	Goetz	28	M	Gregorio	58	M
Giocobo	39	M	Gold	20	M	Gregory	50	M
Giocopo	44	M	Golda	21	F	Greig	37	M
Giorgio	53	M	Goldie	34	F	Gresham	35	M
Giorsal	36	F	Goldsworthy	58	M	Greta	24	F
Giotto	32	M	Goliath	36	M	Gretchen	44	F
Giovanna	56	F	Gomer	31	M	Grete	28	F
Giovanni	64	M	Gomez	30	M	Gretel	31	F
Giraldo	39	M	Gondol	31	M	Gribbon	40	M
Giraud	33	M	Gonzales	36	M	Griffin	51	M
Girra	35	M	Gonzalez	43	M	Griffith	56	M
Girvan	53	M	Goodwin	42	M	Grimaldo	43	M
Gisela	26	F	Goolara	33	F	Grindal	38	M
Giselbert	43	M	Goonagulla	42	M	Grischa	38	M
Gisella	29	F	Goonaroo	46	M	Griselda	39	F
Giselle	33	F	Goraidh	44	M	Gristin	42	F
Gislaine	40	M	Gordi	35	F	Griswold	44	M
Gitana	25	F	Gordon	37	M	Grosvenor	70	M
Githa	27	F	Gore	27	M	Grover	58	M
Gittle	28	F	Gorky	40	M	Grunhilda	49	F
Giuliano	43	M	Gorm	26	M	Gualter	30	M
Giulo	28	M	Gosta	17	M	Gualterio	45	M
Giuseppe	44	M	Gothfraidh	60	M	Gudrun	31	F
Giustina	37	F	Gottfried	50	M	Guglielma	42	F
Giusto	28	M	Gottlieb	36	M	Guglielmo	47	M
Given	48	M	Gottrid	39	M	Guida	24	F
Gladney	32	M	Gough	31	M	Guiditta	37	F
Gladstone	34	M	Gould	23	M	Guido	29	M
Gladwin	34	M	Govinda	54	M	Guilbert	40	M
Gladwyn	32	M	Grace	25	F	Guild	26	M
Gladys	23	F	Grady	28	M	Guillaum	33	M
Gleb	17	M	Graeme	31	M	Guillaume	38	M
Glen	20	M	Grafton	36	M	Guillelmine	56	F
Glenda	25	F	Graham	30	M	Guillermo	49	M
Glenn	25	M	Graine	36	F	Guinevere	70	F
Glenna	26	F	Grande	31	M	Guiseppe	44	M
Glenys	28	F	Granger	43	M	Guiseppina	54	F
Glenyss	29	F	Grant	24	M	Guistino	42	M
Gloria	35	F	Grantham	37	M	Guisto	28	M
Glyn	22	M	Granville	64	M	Gully	23	M
Glynis	32	F	Gray	24	M	Gunnar	30	M
Glynn	27	M	Grayson	36	M	Gunthar	35	M
Godafrey	45	M	Grazina	40	F	Gunther	39	M
Godart	29	M	Greer	35	F	Gupta	20	M
Goddard	35	M	Greg	28	M	Gurion	39	M
Godfrey	44	M	Gregg	35	M	Gustaf	20	M
Godiva	49	F	Gregor	43	M	Gustava	37	F
Godwin	36	M	Gregoria	53	F	Gustave	41	M

Harvey	52	M	Heinz	35	M	Hesper	35	F
Hashir	36	M	Helen	26	F	Hester	30	F
Hashum	25	M	Helena	27	F	Hetty	24	F
Hassan	17	M	Helene	31	F	Heult	21	M
Hastin	26	M	Helenka	38	F	Heulwen	34	F
Hastings	34	M	Helga	24	F	Heutte	25	F
Hathor	34	F	Helianthe	46	F	Hew	18	M
Hati	20	F	Helice	33	F	Hezekiah	55	M
Hattie	27	F	Helier	39	M	Hiawatha	35	M
Hatton	24	M	Heller	20	F	Hibernia	48	F
Hatty	20	F	Hellmut	28	M	Hiew	27	M
Hava	32	F	Helmer	34	M	Hika	29	F
Havelock	59	M	Helmut	25	M	Hikka	40	F
Havgan	44	M	Heloise	37	F	Hilaire	44	M
Hawa	15	F	Helsa	18	F	Hilary	37	B
Haya	17	F	Hemi	26	M	Hilda	25	F
Hayden	30	M	Henare	33	M	Hildegard	50	F
Haydn	25	M	Hendrick	54	M	Hildegarde	55	F
Haydon	31	M	Heng	25	F	Hilderic	50	M
Hayes	22	M	Heni	27	F	Hilliard	46	M
Haylee	29	F	Henri	36	M	Hilma	25	F
Hayley	31	F	Henrietta	46	F	Hilton	33	M
Hayne	26	M	Henriot	44	M	Hina	23	F
Haynes	27	M	Henry	34	M	Hinda	27	F
Hazael	26	M	Heo	19	F	Hine	27	F
Hazel	25	F	Hepetipa	44	M	Hinemoa	38	F
Hazim	30	M	Hera	23	F	Hippocrates	58	M
Hearn	28	M	Herb	24	M	Hiram	31	M
Heath	24	M	Herbert	40	M	Hiria	36	F
Heathcliff	51	M	Herberta	41	F	Hiriwa	41	F
Heathcote	40	M	Hercules	37	M	Hiroko	49	F
Heather	38	F	Herewini	55	M	Hiroshi	50	M
Heaton	27	M	Herman	32	M	Hoa	15	B
Hebe	20	F	Hermando	42	M	Hoang Hgoc	51	F
Heber	29	M	Hermano	38	M	Hobart	28	M
Hector	33	M	Hermes	32	M	Hoda	19	F
Hedda	22	F	Hermia	36	F	Hodaka	31	M
Heddwyn	38	M	Hermine	45	F	Hoel	22	M
Hedley	32	M	Herminia	50	F	Hoibeard	44	M
Hedwig	38	B	Hermione	51	F	Hoireabard	54	M
Hedy	24	F	Hermosa	34	F	Holden	31	M
Heidi	35	F	Hernando	43	M	Holger	38	M
Heiki	42	F	Hero	28	F	Holla	21	F
Heikki	53	M	Herod	32	M	Hollis	30	M
Heilyn	37	M	Herrod	41	M	Holly	27	F
Hein	27	M	Herschel	42	M	Holman	27	M
Heine	32	M	Hertha	33	F	Holmes	27	M
Heinrich	56	M	Herzog	43	M	Holt	19	M

Homer	32	M	Hume	20	M	Ifan	21	M
Homi	27	M	Humphrey	51	M	Igal	20	M
Hone	24	M	Humphry	46	M	Ignacia	35	F
Honesta	28	F	Hung	23	M	Ignacio	40	M
Honey	31	F	Hunt	18	M	Ignascha	35	M
Hong	26	F	Hunter	32	M	Ignatius	37	M
Hong Hgoc	50	F	Huon	22	M	Ignazio	45	M
Honor	34	B	Hurd	24	M	Igor	31	M
Honorata	38	F	Hurley	35	M	Ihakara	40	M
Honoria	44	F	Husha	21	M	Ihorangi	54	M
Hope	26	F	Hushin	34	M	Ihuatamai	38	M
Horace	32	M	Hussain	28	M	Ila	13	F
Horatia	36	F	Hussein	32	M	Ilana	19	F
Horatio	41	M	Huw	16	M	Ilaria	32	F
Horeb	30	F	Huxley	32	M	Ilario	37	M
Hori	32	M	Hyacinth	43	F	Ileana	24	F
Horst	26	M	Hyacintha	44	F	Iliska	34	F
Hortense	41	F	Hyacinthe	48	M	Ilka	24	F
Hosanna	27	F	Hyam	20	M	Illeana	27	F
Hosea	21	M	Hyatt	20	M	Illeane	31	F
Hoshi	32	F	Hyde	24	M	Illiana	31	F
Hotoroa	38	M	Hyman	25	M	Ilona	24	F
Houston	31	M	Hypatia	35	F	Ilone	28	F
Howard	33	M	Hyujong	37	M	Ilsa	14	F
Howe	24	M	Hywel	28	M	Ilse	18	F
Howel	27	M	I Chih	37	M	Imam	18	M
Howell	30	M	Iachimo	40	M	Imber	29	F
Hoyle	29	M	Iacovo	47	M	Imelda	26	F
Hozo	28	M	Iago	23	M	Immanuel	34	M
Hrisoula	40	F	Iain	24	M	Imogen	36	F
Hsia	19	M	Ian	15	M	Imogene	41	F
Hsin	23	M	Ianthe	30	F	Imre	27	M
Hsing	30	M	Ibrahim	42	M	Ina	15	F
Hsuan	18	M	Icabod	25	M	Inara	25	F
Hsuang	25	M	Icarus	26	M	Inari	25	F
Hu	11	M	Ichabod	33	M	Inas	16	F
Huang	24	M	Ichibod	41	M	Indira	37	F
Huatare	29	M	Ida	14	F	Indra	28	M
Hubert	29	M	Idabell	27	F	Indrani	42	F
Huberta	30	F	Idalia	27	F	Indrikus	51	M
Hudd	19	M	Ideal	22	F	Ines	20	F
Hudson	27	M	Idealia	32	F	Inga	22	F
Hue Lan	25	F	Iden	23	M	Ingar	31	F
Huey	23	M	Idetta	23	F	Inge	26	B
Hugh	26	M	Idette	27	F	Ingeborg	50	F
Hughes	32	M	Idona	25	F	Ingemar	40	M
Hugo	24	M	Idris	32	M	Inger	35	M
Hui	20	M	Iduna	22	F	Inglebert	47	M

Ingmar	35	M	Ishmawil	40	M	Izydor	43	M
Ingo	27	M	Isi	19	M	Jaak	14	M
Ingram	35	M	Isidore	43	M	Jabez	17	M
Ingrid	43	F	Isis	20	F	Jace	10	M
Inia	24	M	Iskender	49	M	Jacinda	24	F
Inigo	36	M	Isla	14	F	Jacinta	22	F
Inir	32	M	Isleen	28	F	Jacinth	29	M
Innes	25	M	Ismael	23	M	Jacintha	30	F
Innis	29	M	Ismay	22	F	Jack	16	M
Innocent	40	M	Ismena	25	F	Jackie	30	M
Ino	20	F	Ismene	29	F	Jackson	28	M
Inocenta	36	F	Ismenia	34	F	Jaclyn	20	F
Iola	19	F	Isobel	26	F	Jacob	13	M
Iolanthe	39	F	Isola	20	F	Jacoba	14	F
Iolo	24	M	Isolde	28	F	Jacqueline	43	F
Ion	20	M	Isreal	28	M	Jacques	22	M
Iona	21	F	Issachar	33	M	Jacqui	25	F
Ione	25	F	Issur	23	M	Jade	11	F
Iorwyn	41	M	Istvan	40	M	Jael	10	F
Ira	19	B	Ita	12	F	Jagger	30	M
Irena	29	F	Ithaca	24	F	Jago	15	M
Irene	33	F	Ithel	27	M	Jahdal	18	M
Ireta	26	F	Ithnan	30	M	Jai	11	M
Irfon	35	M	Itta	14	F	Jaime	20	B
Irina	33	F	Ittamar	28	M	Jaimee	25	F
Iris	28	F	Iva	32	B	Jair	20	M
Irja	20	F	Ivan	37	M	Jakab	16	M
Irma	23	F	Ivana	38	F	Jake	18	M
Irmgard	43	F	Ivanjuscha	54	M	Jakk	24	M
Irmin	36	M	Ivanka	49	F	Jakov	41	M
Irmina	37	F	Ivanku	51	F	Jalil	17	M
Irva	41	F	Ivanna	43	F	Jalon	16	M
Irvin	54	M	Ivar	41	M	Jamal	10	M
Irvine	59	M	Iven	41	M	James	12	M
Irving	61	M	Iverna	51	F	Jamie	20	B
Irwin	37	M	Ives	37	B	Jamieson	32	M
Isa	11	B	Ivetta	41	F	Jamin	20	M
Isaac	15	M	Ivette	45	F	Jamina	21	F
Isaak	23	M	Ivka	43	F	Jan	7	B
Isabel	21	F	Ivo	37	M	Jana	8	F
Isabella	25	F	Ivor	46	M	Janda	12	M
Isabelle	29	F	Ivory	53	F	Jane	12	F
Isador	30	M	Ivy	38	F	Janelle	23	F
Isadora	31	F	Iwan	20	M	Janet	14	F
Isaiah	29	M	Izaak	30	M	Janice	24	F
Isambard	31	M	Izabella	32	F	Janine	26	F
Isbel	20	F	Izidora	46	F	Jann	12	M
Ishmael	31	M	Izod	27	M	Jannali	25	F

Joram	21	M	Jurgen	30	M	Kamini	39	F
Jordan	26	M	Jurgi	29	M	Kandelka	41	F
Jordana	27	F	Jussi	15	M	Kane	22	M
Jorg	23	M	Justen	17	M	Kang	24	M
Jorge	28	M	Justice	24	M	Kani	26	F
Joris	26	M	Justin	21	M	Kanku	31	M
Jory	23	M	Justine	26	F	Kanya	25	B
Josaphat	27	M	Justino	27	M	Kao	18	M
Joscelyn	31	F	Justis	17	M	Kaooroo	45	F
Jose	13	M	Jye	13	M	Kara	22	F
Josef	19	M	Jylte	17	F	Karel	29	B
Joselin	30	M	Kaare	27	M	Karen	31	F
Joseph	28	M	Kaarle	30	M	Kari	30	F
Josephine	47	F	Kabir	32	M	Karim	34	M
Josha	17	M	Kacey	27	F	Karin	35	F
Joshua	20	M	Kacha	24	M	Karina	36	F
Josiah	26	M	Kadi	25	F	Karl	24	M
Josie	22	F	Kadla	20	F	Karla	25	F
Josif	23	M	Kae	17	M	Karlee	34	F
Jotham	22	M	Kahla	24	F	Karlin	38	M
Jovita	41	F	Kahlil	35	M	Karlis	34	M
Joy	14	F	Kai	21	M	Karlo	30	M
Joyce	22	F	Kaikasi	43	F	Karly	31	F
Juan	10	M	Kailah	33	F	Karmein	44	F
Juanita	22	F	Kaine	31	M	Karol	30	M
Jubal	10	M	Kaisa	23	F	Karolina	45	F
Jubilee	28	M	Kaitlyn	38	F	Karoline	49	F
Jud	8	M	Kaj	13	M	Karoly	37	M
Judah	17	M	Kakuei	40	M	Karri	39	F
Judas	10	M	Kalah	24	F	Karrin	44	F
Judd	12	M	Kali	24	B	Karsten	34	M
Jude	13	M	Kalid	28	M	Karyn	33	F
Judith	27	F	Kalika	36	F	Kasia	23	F
Judy	15	F	Kalila	28	F	Kasimir	44	M
Jules	13	M	Kalina	30	F	Kasimira	45	F
Julia	17	F	Kalinda	34	F	Kasmira	36	F
Julian	22	M	Kaliope	42	F	Kaspar	30	M
Julianna	23	F	Kalla	19	F	Kasper	34	M
Julie	21	F	Kalyan	28	F	Kassia	24	F
Julien	26	M	Kalypso	36	F	Katalin	32	F
Julienne	36	F	Kama	17	F	Kataraina	40	F
Juliet	23	F	Kamala	21	F	Katarina	39	F
Julio	22	M	Kamaria	36	F	Katarzyna	45	F
Julius	20	M	Kamballa	26	F	Katchen	35	F
June	14	M	Kambara	29	M	Kate	19	F
Junius	22	M	Kameko	38	F	Katelyn	34	F
Juno	15	F	Kamil	28	M	Katerina	43	F
Junus	13	M	Kamilah	37	F	Katharine	51	F

Kathe	27	F	Kelda	24	F	Kester	33	M
Kathel	30	F	Kelham	32	M	Ketura	31	F
Katherina	51	F	Kell	22	M	Kevin	52	M
Katherine	55	F	Keller	36	M	Keyna	29	F
Kathleen	40	F	Kellie	36	F	Keziah	42	F
Kathrina	46	F	Kelly	29	B	Khaled	32	M
Kathrine	50	F	Kelsey	32	B	Khalid	36	M
Kathryn	43	F	Kelso	26	M	Khalif	38	M
Kathy	29	F	Kelvin	55	M	Khalil	35	M
Katia	24	F	Kemal	24	M	Khoung	40	M
Katie	28	F	Kemp	27	M	Kiara	31	F
Katimarie	51	F	Kemper	41	M	Kiel	28	M
Katina	29	F	Ken	21	M	Kieran	40	M
Katinka	40	F	Kendal	29	B	Kiki	40	F
Katra	24	F	Kendall	32	M	Kilian	38	M
Katren	33	F	Kendra	35	F	Kilkie	48	F
Katri	32	F	Kendrick	57	M	Killara	37	F
Katrina	38	F	Kenley	36	M	Killian	41	M
Katrine	42	F	Kenn	26	M	Kim	24	B
Kattie	30	F	Kennard	40	M	Kimba	27	M
Katya	22	F	Kennedy	42	M	Kimbal	30	M
Kauri	33	M	Kenneth	41	M	Kimball	33	B
Kawa	18	M	Kenrick	53	M	Kimbereley	60	F
Kawana	24	F	Kent	23	M	Kimberley	55	B
Kay	19	F	Kentigern	58	M	Kimberly	50	F
Kaye	24	F	Kenton	34	M	Kimiya	41	F
Kayla	23	F	Kenwyn	38	F	Kina	26	M
Kaylah	31	F	Kenyon	39	M	Kindilan	47	F
Kaylea	28	F	Keokuk	47	M	Kineta	33	F
Keal	20	M	Kepler	40	M	King	32	M
Kean	22	M	Kera	26	F	Kinga	33	F
Keane	27	M	Kerekori	65	M	Kingdom	46	M
Keaton	30	M	Keren	35	F	Kingsley	48	M
Kedar	30	M	Kereru	42	M	Kingston	46	M
Kedric	41	M	Kereteki	57	M	Kinnard	44	M
Kee	21	B	Keri	34	F	Kinnell	41	M
Keefe	32	M	Kerill	40	M	Kinnereth	59	F
Keegan	34	B	Kermadec	42	M	Kinnia	40	F
Keelan	30	M	Kermit	40	M	Kinsey	38	M
Keeley	36	M	Kern	30	M	Kinsford	51	M
Keely	31	F	Kerri	43	F	Kinsie	40	F
Keenan	32	M	Kerrie	48	F	Kipp	34	M
Kegan	29	M	Kerry	41	B	Kira	30	F
Keifer	45	M	Kerstan	34	M	Kirby	38	M
Keiko	42	F	Kerstin	42	F	Kiri	38	F
Keir	34	M	Kerttu	32	F	Kirilly	51	F
Keith	35	M	Kerwin	44	M	Kirilyn	53	F
Kelby	28	M	Kesiah	35	F	Kiritin	54	M

Kirk	40	M	Koppel	39	M	Kuoni	34	M
Kirkwood	61	M	Kora	27	F	Kupe	26	M
Kirli	41	F	Kordula	37	F	Kura	24	B
Kirra	39	F	Koren	36	F	Kuracca	31	M
Kirri	47	F	Kornelia	49	F	Kurao	30	M
Kirstel	40	F	Kornelius	52	M	Kurd	27	M
Kirsten	42	F	Korong	44	M	Kurmoonah	53	F
Kirstie	46	F	Kort	28	M	Kurnkuni	56	M
Kirstin	46	F	Kosmas	24	M	Kurrawa	39	M
Kirsty	39	F	Kotka	31	B	Kurt	25	M
Kit	22	B	Kourapapa	46	M	Kuyan	27	M
Kitri	40	F	Kris	30	M	Kwan	22	F
Kitty	31	F	Krishna	44	M	Kyla	22	F
Klaas	17	M	Krisian	45	M	Kyle	26	M
Klara	25	F	Krispin	51	M	Kylie	35	F
Klaudia	32	F	Krista	33	F	Kylli	33	F
Klaus	19	M	Kristal	36	F	Kym	22	B
Klemens	34	M	Kristel	40	F	Kyna	24	F
Klemin	37	M	Kristen	42	F	Kyne	28	M
Klemmens	38	M	Krister	46	M	Kyrena	38	F
Kliment	39	M	Kristin	46	F	Kyril	39	M
Klinger	49	M	Kristina	47	F	Kyrus	31	M
Knight	42	M	Kristine	51	F	Laban	12	M
Knox	28	M	Kristle	40	F	Labhaoise	36	F
Knud	23	M	Kristof	44	M	Labhras	25	M
Knut	21	M	Kristofer	58	M	Labhruinn	45	M
Ko	17	M	Kristopher	67	M	Lace	12	F
Koba	20	F	Kristy	39	F	Lacey	19	F
Kobai	29	M	Krita	32	F	Lach	15	M
Kodai	31	F	Krys	28	F	Lachlan	24	M
Koenraad	42	M	Krysta	31	F	Lachman	25	M
Kogarah	43	F	Krystal	34	F	Lacy	14	M
Kohia	35	F	Krysten	40	F	Ladislas	23	M
Koiranah	50	M	Krystle	38	F	Lael	12	M
Kokomis	48	F	Ku	14	M	Lagana	18	F
Kolet	27	M	Kuang	27	M	Laibrook	47	M
Koleyn	37	M	Kudno	29	M	Lain	18	M
Kolora	36	F	Kuei	28	B	Lainey	30	F
Kolya	28	M	Kuini	37	F	Laing	25	M
Koninderie	68	F	Kulka	29	F	Laird	26	M
Kono	28	F	Kum	18	M	Lajos	12	M
Konrad	36	M	Kumari	37	F	Lakkari	45	F
Konstancia	44	F	Kumbelin	42	F	Lako	21	M
Konstantin	47	M	Kumera	33	M	Lala	8	F
Konstanze	44	F	Kunaama	26	F	Lalage	20	F
Koo	23	F	Kunama	25	F	Lalita	19	F
Koolyoo	45	M	Kung	26	M	Lalota	16	F
Koora	33	F	Kuo	20	M	Lamar	18	M

Letha	19	F	Lindsay	30	B	Lois	19	F
Leticia	32	F	Lindsey	34	B	Lola	13	F
Letitia	31	F	Lindy	28	F	Lolita	24	F
Lettice	29	F	Linet	24	F	Lolly	22	F
Leupold	31	M	Linette	31	F	Loma	14	F
Leura	21	F	Linley	32	B	Lombard	29	M
Levana	37	F	Linnea	28	F	Lombardo	35	M
Levi	39	M	Linnet	29	F	Lon	14	M
Levina	45	F	Linton	30	M	Lona	15	F
Lew	13	M	Linus	21	M	Loni	23	F
Lewanna	25	F	Lion	23	M	Lonie	28	F
Lewis	23	M	Lionardo	43	M	Lonnie	33	F
Lex	14	M	Lionel	31	M	Lora	19	F
Li	12	B	Liong	30	M	Lore	23	F
Liam	17	M	Lior	27	M	Lorelei	40	F
Liana	19	F	Liorah	36	F	Lorelle	34	F
Libby	23	F	Lira	22	F	Lorelly	36	F
Libero	34	M	Lirralirra	62	F	Loren	28	B
Liberty	37	F	Lis	13	F	Lorena	29	F
Libusa	19	F	Lisa	14	F	Lorenco	37	M
Lida	17	F	Lisbeth	30	F	Lorenz	36	M
Lide	21	F	Lisette	27	F	Lorenzo	42	M
Lief	23	M	Lisle	21	B	Loretta	28	F
Lila	16	F	Liso	19	F	Lori	27	F
Lilac	19	F	Lissa	15	F	Lorimer	45	M
Lilah	24	F	Lister	29	M	Lorin	32	M
Lili	24	F	Lita	15	F	Loring	39	M
Lilian	30	F	Liu	15	M	Lorna	24	F
Lilie	29	F	Liv	34	F	Lorne	28	M
Lilith	34	F	Livia	44	F	Lorraine	47	F
Lilla	19	F	Livingstone	74	M	Losaline	33	F
Lilli	27	F	Liz	20	F	Lotta	14	F
Lillian	33	F	Liza	21	F	Lotte	18	F
Lillipilli	58	F	Lizanne	36	F	Lottie	27	F
Lilly	25	F	Lizette	34	F	Lotus	15	F
Lily	22	F	Lizzy	35	F	Lou	12	F
Lim	16	M	Ljubica	22	F	Louella	24	F
Lin	17	B	Llawela	21	F	Loughlin	44	M
Lina	18	F	Lleufer	34	M	Louis	22	M
Lincoln	34	M	Llewella	28	F	Louisa	23	F
Lind	21	B	Llewellyn	39	M	Louise	27	F
Linda	22	F	Llewelyn	36	M	Lourenco	40	M
Lindal	25	F	Lloyd	23	M	Love	36	F
Lindall	28	F	Lloydice	40	F	Loveday	48	F
Lindberg	44	M	Loch	20	M	Lowana	21	F
Linden	31	B	Lockwood	44	M	Lowanna	26	F
Lindley	36	M	Logan	22	M	Lowell	25	M
Lindon	32	M	Lolla	22	F	Lowrie	37	M

Loyce	24	F	Lycidas	28	M	Maddox	25	M
Loyd	20	M	Lycon	24	M	Madeleine	41	F
Luana	13	F	Lycurgus	36	M	Madeline	36	F
Luba	9	F	Lydia	24	F	Madge	21	F
Lubin	22	M	Lyell	21	M	Madira	28	F
Luc	9	M	Lyle	18	M	Madison	30	M
Luca	10	M	Lyman	20	M	Madlena	23	F
Lucas	11	M	Lyn	15	F	Madoc	18	M
Luce	14	F	Lyncus	22	M	Madon	20	M
Lucelle	25	F	Lynda	20	F	Madonna	26	F
Lucia	19	F	Lyndal	23	F	Madra	19	F
Luciana	25	F	Lyndon	30	M	Madri	27	F
Luciano	30	M	Lynelle	31	F	Mae	10	F
Lucie	23	F	Lynette	29	F	Maelgwyn	37	M
Lucien	28	M	Lynfa	22	M	Maelle	21	F
Lucille	29	F	Lynn	20	B	Magali	25	F
Lucina	24	B	Lynne	25	F	Magda	17	F
Lucinda	28	F	Lynnette	34	F	Magdalen	30	F
Lucippe	37	M	Lynton	28	M	Magdalena	31	F
Lucretia	35	F	Lynus	19	M	Magdelen	34	F
Lucy	16	F	Lynwood	36	M	Magdelene	39	F
Ludger	31	M	Lyonel	29	M	Maggie	33	F
Ludlow	24	M	Lyonelle	37	F	Magnolia	36	F
Ludolf	25	M	Lyra	20	F	Magnus	21	M
Ludovika	59	F	Lyris	29	F	Maguire	38	M
Ludvig	48	M	Lysander	35	M	Mahala	18	F
Ludwig	31	M	Lysandra	31	F	Mahalia	27	F
Ludwiga	32	F	Lystra	23	F	Mahes	19	M
Luella	18	F	Lytton	25	M	Mahla	17	F
Lugaidh	35	M	Lyulf	22	M	Mahlon	27	M
Luigi	31	M	Maarten	27	M	Mahmud	24	M
Luis	16	M	Mab	7	F	Mahon	24	M
Luisa	17	F	Mabel	15	F	Mahra	23	F
Luise	21	F	Mabella	19	F	Mahuika	37	F
Luitpold	37	M	Mabon	18	M	Mahura	26	F
Luiz	23	M	Mac	8	M	Mahuru	28	F
Luka	18	B	Macarius	31	M	Mai	14	F
Luke	22	M	Macey	20	M	Maia	15	F
Lulu	12	F	Macfarlane	38	M	Maicaela	27	F
Lupe	18	F	Macharios	42	M	Maida	19	F
Lupus	17	M	Mack	19	M	Maighdlin	50	F
Lurline	37	F	Mackenzie	51	M	Maillard	34	F
Lute	13	F	Macnair	32	M	Mair	23	F
Luthais	27	M	Macpherson	49	M	Maire	28	F
Luther	30	M	Macy	15	M	Mairghread	57	F
Luz	14	F	Madalena	24	F	Maitland	29	M
Luzian	29	M	Madde	18	F	Maja	7	F
Lyall	17	M	Maddock	33	M	Major	21	M

Maka	17	M	Marcellus	32	M	Marita	26	F
Makarios	42	M	Marcia	27	F	Marius	27	M
Makitaka	40	M	Marco	23	M	Marjorie	44	F
Malachi	29	M	Marcos	24	M	Marjory	37	F
Malchi	28	M	Marcus	21	M	Mark	25	M
Malchus	23	M	Mardi	27	F	Markku	39	M
Malcolm	24	M	Mardia	28	F	Marko	31	M
Malena	19	F	Marea	20	F	Markos	32	M
Malinda	27	F	Maree	24	F	Marla	18	F
Malise	23	M	Marei	28	F	Marlee	27	F
Mallard	25	M	Mareiel	36	F	Marlen	27	M
Mallory	33	B	Marek	30	M	Marlene	32	F
Malone	24	M	Marelda	27	F	Marley	29	M
Maloney	31	M	Maresa	21	F	Marli	26	F
Malory	30	M	Marette	28	F	Marline	36	F
Malva	31	F	Margaret	38	F	Marlon	28	M
Malvin	44	M	Margarita	43	F	Marlow	28	M
Malvina	45	F	Margarite	47	F	Marmion	38	M
Mame	14	F	Margarta	34	F	Marney	31	F
Mamie	23	F	Margaux	31	F	Marnie	33	F
Manasseh	26	M	Margen	31	F	Marnin	33	M
Manchu	24	M	Margery	42	F	Maroo	26	F
Mancia	23	F	Margo	27	F	Marsden	29	M
Mandel	22	M	Margot	29	F	Marsh	23	M
Mander	28	M	Margreta	38	F	Marsha	24	M
Mandu	17	M	Margrete	42	F	Marshall	30	M
Mandy	21	F	Margriet	46	F	Marta	17	F
Manfred	34	M	Marguerite	54	F	Marten	26	M
Manka	22	F	Mari	23	F	Martha	25	F
Manley	25	M	Maria	24	F	Martin	30	M
Manly	20	M	Mariam	28	F	Martina	31	F
Manning	36	M	Marian	29	F	Martine	35	F
Manoah	25	M	Mariana	30	F	Maru	17	F
Manoel	24	M	Mariane	34	F	Marvin	50	M
Manolis	29	M	Marianne	39	F	Mary	21	F
Manon	21	F	Marie	28	F	Maryanne	37	F
Manrico	37	M	Mariel	31	F	Maryjane	33	F
Mansfield	38	M	Mariequita	51	F	Marylou	33	F
Manuel	21	M	Marietje	36	F	Maryse	27	F
Manuela	22	F	Marietta	33	F	Mascot	17	M
Manuelita	33	F	Marigold	43	F	Masorah	30	M
Mara	15	F	Marilyn	38	F	Massimiliano	53	M
Marah	23	F	Marina	29	F	Massimo	26	M
Marama	20	M	Marino	34	M	Mata	8	M
Marc	17	M	Mario	29	M	Mataora	24	M
Marcel	25	M	Marion	34	B	Matareka	34	M
Marcella	29	F	Maris	24	F	Mate	12	M
Marcello	34	M	Marise	29	F	Math	15	M

Mathena	26	F	Medina	28	F	Mercede	35	F
Mathias	26	M	Medora	29	F	Mercedes	36	F
Mathilda	32	F	Medwenna	34	F	Mercer	35	M
Matilda	24	F	Medwin	32	M	Mercia	31	F
Matiu	19	M	Mee	14	F	Mercurino	53	M
Matong	25	M	Meegan	27	F	Mercy	28	F
Matt	9	M	Meg	16	F	Mere	23	M
Mattea	15	F	Megan	22	F	Meredith	46	F
Matthew	27	M	Meghan	30	F	Meriki	43	F
Matthias	28	M	Mehitabel	39	F	Meridee	41	F
Matui	19	M	Mei	18	F	Merinda	37	F
Maud	12	F	Mei Kuei	46	F	Merivale	58	M
Maude	17	F	Mei Yu	28	F	Merle	26	F
Maui	17	B	Mel	12	M	Merlin	35	M
Maura	18	F	Melania	28	F	Merlyn	33	M
Maureen	32	F	Melanie	32	F	Merrilees	50	F
Maurice	34	M	Melantha	29	F	Merrill	42	M
Maurilla	33	F	Melany	25	F	Merry	34	F
Maurizia	44	F	Melba	15	F	Merryn	39	F
Mauve	35	F	Melbourne	42	M	Merton	31	M
Mave	32	F	Melchior	47	M	Meru	21	F
Mavis	37	F	Melea	18	M	Merv	40	M
Max	11	M	Melia	22	F	Mervin	54	M
Maxim	24	M	Melina	26	F	Mervyn	52	M
Maxima	25	F	Melinda	31	F	Meryl	28	F
Maximilian	51	M	Melior	36	F	Meshullam	32	M
Maximilien	55	M	Melisande	37	F	Messina	26	F
Maximillian	54	M	Melissa	24	F	Mestra	22	F
Maximin	38	M	Melita	24	F	Meta	12	F
Maxine	30	F	Mellisa	26	F	Methuselah	40	M
Maxwell	27	M	Melmoth	32	M	Meyer	30	M
May	12	F	Melody	29	F	Mia	14	F
Maya	13	F	Melony	30	F	Miao	20	F
Maybelle	30	F	Melrosa	29	F	Micah	25	B
Mayer	26	M	Melrose	33	M	Michael	33	M
Mayfield	39	M	Melva	35	F	Michaela	34	F
Mayhew	30	M	Melvia	44	F	Michal	28	F
Maynard	31	M	Melville	54	M	Michel	32	M
Mayo	18	M	Melvin	48	M	Michele	37	F
Mayra	22	F	Melvyn	46	M	Michelina	47	F
Mayrah	30	F	Menachem	35	M	Micheline	51	F
McCadie	29	F	Menachin	40	M	Michelle	40	F
Mead	14	M	Menchem	34	M	Michi	33	F
Meade	19	M	Mendel	26	M	Mick	27	M
Meara	20	F	Menes	20	M	Mickey	39	M
Meave	37	F	Menia	24	F	Midas	19	M
Meda	14	F	Menna	20	F	Midgee	34	M
Media	23	F	Merari	37	F	Mie	18	F

Mieke	34	F	Minka	30	F	Monroe	35	M
Mignon	36	F	Minkie	43	F	Montague	33	M
Miguel	31	M	Minna	24	F	Monte	22	M
Miguela	32	F	Minnette	37	F	Montgomery	55	M
Miguelita	43	F	Minnie	37	F	Moondara	36	F
Mihai	31	M	Minore	38	F	Moorang	38	F
Miharo	37	M	Minos	25	M	Morag	27	F
Mija	15	F	Mintha	29	F	Mordecai	41	M
Mike	29	M	Minu	21	F	Moree	29	F
Mikhail	45	M	Minya	26	F	Moreen	34	F
Mikhaila	46	F	Mira	23	F	Moreno	35	M
Mikko	41	M	Mirabel	33	F	Morgan	32	B
Miklos	34	M	Miranda	33	F	Morgana	33	F
Mila	17	F	Mireille	47	F	Moria	29	F
Milan	22	M	Mirella	34	F	Moriah	37	M
Milburn	35	M	Miriam	36	F	Morina	34	F
Milcah	28	F	Mirko	39	M	Moritz	38	M
Milda	21	F	Miroslav	55	M	Morley	34	M
Mildred	38	F	Mirria	41	F	Morna	25	F
Miles	22	M	Mirrin	45	F	Moroto	33	M
Milford	41	M	Mischa	26	M	Morrell	39	M
Milicia	38	F	Mishael	31	M	Morris	38	M
Milka	28	F	Mitchell	37	M	Morrison	49	M
Millar	29	M	Mitiaro	40	M	Mort	21	M
Millard	33	M	Mitra	25	F	Mortimer	48	M
Millemurro	55	F	Mitzi	32	F	Morton	32	M
Miller	33	M	Mladen	22	M	Morven	51	M
Millett	28	M	Modeste	27	M	Mosera	26	F
Milli	28	F	Modestine	41	F	Moses	17	M
Millicent	43	F	Modesty	29	F	Moshe	24	M
Millington	53	M	Modred	32	M	Mosina	26	F
Millissa	31	F	Modwen	29	F	Moulton	29	M
Milly	26	F	Moelwyn	35	M	Mountbatten	37	M
Milner	35	M	Moesen	26	M	Mowantyi	39	M
Milo	22	M	Moffatt	27	M	Moya	18	F
Milosov	49	M	Mohammed	36	M	Mozelle	34	F
Miltiades	38	M	Moibeal	30	F	Muhammad	29	M
Milton	29	M	Moira	29	F	Muir	25	M
Mimi	26	F	Moireach	45	F	Muire	30	F
Mimosa	25	F	Moise	25	M	Muirhead	43	M
Mina	19	F	Mokoiro	51	M	Mulga	18	M
Minamberang	52	F	Molan	19	M	Mullaya	22	M
Minella	30	F	Molly	23	F	Mullion	33	M
Minerva	55	F	Mona	16	F	Muna	13	F
Minet	25	M	Monette	29	F	Mungo	25	M
Minette	32	F	Monica	28	F	Munro	27	M
Ming	25	M	Monika	36	F	Mura	17	M
Minh	26	M	Monique	40	F	Muralappi	44	F

Murdoch	37	M	Nama	11	F	Neal	14	M
Muriel	33	F	Nambur	24	M	Neala	15	F
Murna	22	F	Nan	11	F	Neco	19	M
Murphy	38	B	Nana	12	F	Ned	14	M
Murray	33	M	Nance	19	F	Neda	15	F
Murrembooee	58	M	Nancy	21	F	Neddy	25	M
Murrumbung	49	M	Nancye	26	F	Neerim	37	M
Murtagh	34	M	Nanda	16	F	Nehemiah	45	M
Musa	9	B	Nandalie	33	F	Neil	22	M
Musetta	18	F	Nanette	25	F	Nelda	18	F
Muzio	30	M	Nani	20	F	Nelia	23	F
Mwynen	31	F	Nanna	17	F	Nell	16	F
Myall	18	M	Nannos	23	M	Nellie	30	F
Mycroft	37	M	Naomi	25	F	Nelson	25	M
Myee	21	F	Naphtali	36	M	Nelwyn	30	F
Myfanwy	35	F	Napier	36	M	Nemo	20	M
Myimbarr	45	M	Napoleon	38	M	Neola	20	F
Myles	20	M	Nara	16	F	Neoma	21	F
Myra	21	F	Narayan	29	M	Nereus	28	M
Myrna	26	F	Narbethong	50	F	Nerida	33	F
Myron	31	M	Narda	20	F	Nerima	33	F
Myrtle	30	F	Nardoo	31	B	Nerina	34	F
Myuna	20	F	Narelle	31	F	Nerine	38	F
Na'amah	20	F	Narn	20	M	Nerissa	31	F
Naaman	17	M	Narrawa	31	F	Nero	25	M
Naarah	25	F	Nartee	27	F	Neroli	37	F
Naarai	26	M	Nastassia	22	F	Nerva	42	M
Naashom	26	F	Nastasya	19	F	Neryl	29	F
Naatja	11	F	Nastaya	18	F	Nerys	27	F
Nada	11	F	Naste	14	F	Nessie	26	F
Nadale	19	F	Nastyenka	38	F	Nesta	14	F
Nadda	15	F	Nata	9	F	Nestor	28	M
Nadege	27	F	Natal	12	M	Netta	15	F
Nadel	18	F	Natale	17	F	Nettie	28	F
Nadelle	26	F	Natalia	22	F	Neumann	28	M
Nadia	20	F	Natalie	26	F	Neva	33	F
Nadine	29	F	Natasha	19	F	Neville	52	M
Naeem	20	M	Natham	21	M	Nevin	46	M
Nafanael	27	M	Nathan	21	M	Newbold	30	M
Nahshon	34	M	Nathanael	31	M	Newbury	36	M
Nahum	21	M	Nathania	32	F	Newell	26	M
Naida	20	F	Nathaniel	39	M	Newlin	32	M
Nain	20	M	Natividad	57	F	Newton	28	M
Nairn	29	M	Natlia	21	F	Neysa	19	F
Nakkare	43	F	Natoma	19	F	Ngahere	40	F
Nala	10	M	Natsha	18	F	Ngahue	29	M
Naldo	19	M	Natuska	24	F	Ngaio	28	F
Naliandrah	46	F	Naylor	31	M	Ngaire	36	F

Name	No.	Sex	Name	No.	Sex	Name	No.	Sex
Ngaroariki	67	F	Ninus	23	M	Nunkalowe	44	F
Ngaru	25	M	Nirah	32	F	Nunkeri	47	F
Nghia	30	M	Niree	33	F	Nunkumbil	45	F
Ngoc	21	F	Nissa	17	F	Nurla	21	F
Ngoc Lan	30	F	Nita	17	F	Nuvarahu	52	F
Ngoc Nhan	40	F	Nitya	24	M	Nyah	21	F
Ngoc Nu	29	F	Nixie	34	F	Nydia	26	F
Nguen	25	F	Nixon	31	M	Nye	17	M
Nguon	26	F	Noah	20	M	Nymbin	32	M
Ngutuku	34	M	Noam	16	M	Nympha	32	F
Nguyen	32	M	Noble	21	M	Nyomi	31	F
Nial	18	M	Noel	19	B	Nyora	28	F
Niall	21	M	Noelda	21	F	Nyrang	34	F
Nicander	41	M	Noeline	38	F	Nyree	31	F
Nicholas	36	M	Noelle	27	F	Nysa	14	F
Nico	23	M	Nohah	28	M	Nyssa	15	F
Nicodemus	40	M	Noilani	38	F	Oake	23	F
Nicol	26	M	Nola	15	F	Oakley	33	M
Nicola	27	F	Nolan	20	M	Oata	10	M
Nicolas	28	M	Nolana	21	F	Obadiah	31	M
Nicolaus	31	M	Nolene	29	F	Obed	17	M
Nicole	31	F	Noleta	22	F	Obelia	26	F
Nicolette	40	F	Nona	17	F	Oberon	33	M
Nicomede	41	M	Noni	25	F	Obert	24	M
Nicomedes	42	M	Noora	27	F	Obrien	36	M
Nidda	23	F	Nora	21	F	Oconnor	40	M
Nidra	28	F	Norah	29	F	Octave	39	M
Niels	23	M	Norbert	38	M	Octavia	44	F
Nigel	29	M	Noris	30	M	Octavie	48	F
Nike	30	F	Norley	35	M	Octavius	47	M
Nikita	37	M	Norma	25	F	Odelette	32	F
Nikka	37	M	Norman	30	M	Odelia	28	F
Nikki	45	F	Norna	26	F	Odell	21	F
Niklas	30	M	Norris	39	M	Odessa	18	F
Nikolaus	39	M	Norton	33	M	Odette	24	F
Niku	28	M	Norvall	49	M	Odile	27	F
Nila	18	F	Norville	62	M	Odilia	32	F
Niles	23	M	Norvin	56	M	Odilon	33	M
Nili	26	F	Norwin	39	M	Odolf	25	M
Nils	18	M	Norwood	41	M	Odwin	29	M
Nilton	30	M	Nouri	32	M	Oeneus	25	M
Nimrod	37	M	Nova	34	F	Ofrah	30	F
Nina	20	F	Novla	43	F	Ogden	27	M
Ninbin	35	M	Nowell	27	M	Ogier	36	M
Ninette	33	F	Nu	8	F	Ogilvie	61	M
Ninian	34	M	Nuala	13	F	Ohini	41	F
Nino	25	M	Nui	17	M	Okeefe	38	M
Ninon	30	F	Nunciata	29	F	Ola	10	F

Pagan	21	B	Paschal	24	M	Pelion	35	M
Page	20	B	Paschasia	32	F	Pell	18	M
Paget	22	M	Pascoe	23	M	Pelton	28	M
Paige	29	B	Pasquale	29	M	Pembroke	49	M
Paine	27	M	Pasquette	34	F	Penda	22	M
Painton	35	M	Pati	19	M	Pendle	29	M
Paley	23	M	Patience	37	F	Penelope	43	F
Pallas	16	F	Paton	21	M	Penia	27	F
Palm	15	F	Patrice	36	F	Penina	32	F
Palma	16	F	Patricia	41	F	Peninah	40	F
Palmer	29	M	Patrick	42	M	Penn	22	M
Palmira	34	F	Patroclus	35	M	Penny	29	F
Palmiro	39	M	Patsy	18	F	Penrith	45	M
Paloma	22	F	Patti	21	F	Penrod	36	M
Pamela	21	F	Patton	23	M	Penrose	38	M
Pamina	27	F	Patty	19	F	Penthea	33	F
Pan	13	M	Patu	13	M	Penwyn	34	M
Panacea	23	F	Patya	18	F	Peony	30	F
Panayiotos	45	M	Paul	14	M	Peospero	46	M
Pancras	27	M	Paula	15	F	Pepe	24	M
Pandora	33	F	Paulette	28	F	Pepilla	35	F
Pandu	20	M	Paulin	28	M	Pepin	33	M
Pania	23	F	Paulina	29	F	Pepita	31	F
Pansy	21	F	Pauline	33	F	Per	21	M
Panthea	29	F	Paulino	34	M	Percival	59	M
Paola	18	F	Paulo	20	M	Percy	31	M
Paolo	23	M	Pavel	38	M	Perde	30	F
Paora	24	M	Pavla	34	F	Perdita	37	F
Papa	16	M	Paxton	27	M	Peregrin	56	M
Papatuanuki	50	M	Payne	25	M	Peregrina	57	F
Paques	25	F	Payton	28	M	Peregrine	61	M
Paramahansa	39	M	Paz	16	F	Perette	35	F
Paree	27	F	Peace	21	F	Perez	34	M
Paris	27	B	Peach	24	F	Pericles	42	M
Parker	42	M	Peaches	30	F	Peridot	42	F
Parkin	42	M	Peadair	36	M	Perilla	37	F
Parlan	26	M	Pearl	25	F	Periot	38	F
Parnel	30	F	Peata	16	F	Perlita	36	F
Parnell	33	M	Peder	30	M	Pernella	38	F
Parnella	34	F	Pedro	31	M	Pernelle	42	F
Parnelle	38	F	Peg	19	F	Pero	27	M
Parr	26	M	Peggy	33	F	Peronel	40	F
Parrell	37	M	Pejo	19	M	Peronne	42	F
Parri	35	M	Pekeri	46	F	Perpetua	39	F
Parry	33	M	Pekka	35	M	Perrin	44	M
Parthenia	47	F	Pelagia	33	F	Perry	37	B
Pascal	16	M	Pelham	28	M	Persephone	58	F
Pascha	21	F	Pelias	26	M	Persia	32	F

Perth	31	M	Phyllis	38	F	Pomona	29	F
Peta	15	F	Pia	17	F	Pontius	33	M
Petar	24	M	Pickford	55	M	Poppy	34	F
Peter	28	M	Picton	32	M	Porter	38	M
Petica	27	F	Pier	30	B	Portia	34	F
Petra	24	F	Pierce	38	M	Poul	19	M
Petrina	38	F	Pierina	45	F	Powell	29	M
Petronella	46	F	Piero	36	M	Powys	26	M
Petronilla	50	F	Pierre	44	M	Prahnee	40	F
Petros	30	M	Piers	31	M	Pramana	28	M
Petula	21	F	Piet	23	M	Prentice	45	M
Petunia	32	F	Pieter	37	M	Prentiss	39	M
Phaedora	41	F	Pietro	38	M	Prescott	35	M
Phanessa	29	F	Pikuwa	36	M	Preston	35	M
Phanuel	32	M	Pilar	29	F	Prewitt	39	M
Pharamond	45	M	Pileb	26	M	Price	33	M
Phebe	27	F	Pilita	31	F	Prima	30	F
Phedra	34	F	Piltti	32	F	Primavera	67	F
Phedre	38	F	Pinterry	53	F	Primo	35	M
Phelan	29	M	Piotr	33	M	Primrose	50	F
Phelp	30	M	Piper	37	F	Prince	38	M
Phelps	31	M	Pipipa	40	F	Prioska	44	F
Phemie	38	F	Pippa	31	F	Priscilla	45	F
Philadelphia	65	F	Piran	31	M	Probus	28	M
Philana	34	F	Pirramurar	61	M	Prosper	44	M
Philantha	44	F	Pirrit	45	F	Prudence	41	F
Philaret	44	M	Pita	19	M	Prudent	35	M
Philbert	45	M	Pitney	35	M	Prue	24	F
Philberta	46	F	Pitt	20	M	Prunella	36	F
Philemina	51	F	Pixie	36	F	Psyche	31	F
Philemon	47	M	Placid	27	M	Puillian	40	M
Philetas	36	F	Placidia	37	F	Pulcheria	48	F
Philiman	46	M	Placido	33	M	Puriri	46	M
Philip	43	M	Plato	19	M	Pyrena	34	F
Philipp	50	M	Platt	15	M	Pythagoras	49	M
Philippa	51	F	Pleasance	31	F	Pythia	34	F
Philippe	55	M	Pleasant	25	F	Qadir	31	M
Phillida	44	F	Pola	17	F	Quabiz	31	M
Philo	33	M	Pollard	33	M	Quahhar	38	M
Philomena	48	F	Pollock	39	M	Quamby	25	M
Philothea	49	F	Polly	26	F	Quarrallia	47	F
Phineas	36	M	Pollyanna	38	F	Qubilah	34	F
Phoebe	33	F	Polonia	37	F	Queanbeyan	42	F
Phoebus	32	M	Polyzena	42	F	Quebec	26	F
Photina	38	F	Poma	18	F	Queenie	40	F
Phuc	21	M	Pomare	32	M	Quelita	31	F
Phung	30	F	Pomeroy	44	M	Quenby	30	F
Phuong	36	B	Pomme	26	F	Quenes	27	M

Quennel	34	M	Raimund	35	M	Rayma	22	F
Quentin	37	M	Raina	25	F	Raymond	36	M
Querida	39	F	Raine	29	F	Rayner	36	M
Queron	36	M	Rainier	47	M	Raynor	37	M
Quieta	28	F	Raissa	22	F	Reamonn	35	M
Quigley	42	M	Raja	12	M	Rebecah	33	F
Quillam	40	M	Raleigh	42	M	Rebecca	28	F
Quillan	32	M	Ralph	28	M	Rebekka	44	F
Quiller	40	M	Ralston	27	M	Rechaba	29	F
Quimby	33	M	Rama	15	M	Red	18	M
Quincey	40	M	Rames	20	M	Redmond	36	M
Quincy	35	M	Ramiah	32	M	Redmund	34	M
Quinlan	34	M	Ramon	25	M	Reece	27	M
Quinn	30	M	Ramona	26	F	Reed	23	M
Quinta	28	F	Ramsay	23	M	Reg	21	M
Quintina	42	F	Ramsey	27	M	Regan	27	B
Quinton	38	M	Ran	15	M	Regina	36	F
Quintus	31	M	Rana	16	F	Reginald	43	M
Quiric	41	M	Ranalt	21	F	Regis	31	M
Quirinus	47	M	Rand	19	M	Reid	27	M
Quiteria	46	F	Randal	23	M	Reidun	35	F
Quoda	22	F	Randall	26	M	Reilly	36	M
Raama	16	F	Randolf	34	M	Reina	29	F
Rabia	22	F	Randolph	43	M	Reinald	36	M
Rachael	30	F	Randy	26	B	Reinaldo	42	M
Rachel	29	F	Ranee	25	F	Reine	33	F
Rachelle	37	F	Ranelle	31	F	Reinhard	50	M
Radburn	33	M	Ranger	36	M	Reinwald	41	M
Radcliffe	36	M	Rangi	31	B	Remi	27	M
Radella	26	F	Rani	24	F	Remington	52	M
Radford	39	M	Ranier	38	M	Remo	24	M
Radha	23	F	Raoghnailt	51	F	Remus	22	M
Radinka	40	F	Raoul	22	M	Remy	25	M
Radley	29	M	Raphaeia	41	F	Rena	20	F
Radmilla	34	F	Raphael	34	M	Renaldo	33	M
Rae	15	B	Raquel	29	F	Renard	33	M
Raelene	33	F	Rashid	32	M	Renata	23	F
Raeline	37	F	Rasia	21	F	Renato	28	M
Rafael	25	M	Rasma	16	F	Renaud	27	M
Raffalella	38	F	Rasmussen	30	M	Renault	28	M
Rafferty	45	M	Rata	13	M	Renay	27	F
Rafu	19	M	Raul	16	M	Rene	24	B
Raghnall	37	M	Rawiri	42	M	Renee	29	F
Ragnar	32	M	Ray	17	B	Renita	31	F
Ragnhild	46	F	Rayburn	36	M	Renny	31	F
Ragnor	37	M	Raydon	32	M	Rere	28	F
Rahel	26	F	Raye	22	F	Resa	16	F
Rahul	24	M	Rayleigh	49	M	Reseda	25	F

Reta	17	F	Richie	43	M	Rochelle	42	F
Reuben	29	M	Richmond	48	M	Rochester	48	M
Rewa	20	F	Rick	32	M	Rock	29	M
Rewuri	40	F	Ricky	39	M	Rockwell	45	M
Rex	20	M	Ridgley	44	M	Rocky	36	M
Rexana	27	F	Ridley	37	M	Rod	19	M
Rey	21	M	Rieke	39	F	Roden	29	M
Reynard	40	M	Rigby	34	M	Roderica	46	F
Reynold	39	M	Rigg	32	M	Roderick	56	M
Rhain	32	M	Rikki	49	F	Rodger	40	M
Rhea	23	F	Riley	33	M	Rodhlann	41	M
Rhedyn	38	F	Rilla	25	F	Rodney	36	M
Rheese	33	M	Rilta	24	F	Rodolf	34	M
Rheinhold	57	M	Rima	23	F	Rodolfo	40	M
Rheta	25	F	Rimu	25	F	Rodolph	43	M
Rhett	26	M	Rina	24	F	Rodway	32	M
Rhiain	41	F	Rinah	32	F	Roeland	33	M
Rhianne	42	F	Rinaldo	37	M	Roesia	31	F
Rhiannon	48	F	Ringbalin	50	M	Rogan	28	M
Rhianwen	47	F	Ringo	36	M	Roger	36	M
Rhianydd	47	F	Rio	24	M	Rohan	29	M
Rhidian	45	M	Riobard	40	M	Rohana	30	F
Rhina	32	F	Riona	30	F	Rois	25	F
Rhoda	28	F	Riordan	43	M	Roland	28	M
Rhodanthe	48	F	Riordon	48	M	Rolanda	29	F
Rhodeia	42	F	Rip	25	M	Rolf	24	M
Rhodope	45	F	Ripley	40	M	Rollo	27	M
Rhona	29	F	Risa	20	F	Rolo	24	M
Rhonda	33	F	Rise	24	F	Roma	20	F
Rhondda	37	F	Rita	21	F	Romain	34	M
Rhonwen	43	F	Ritza	29	F	Roman	25	M
Rhun	25	M	Riva	41	F	Romana	26	F
Rhydwyn	45	M	Rizpah	42	F	Romania	35	F
Rhyl	27	F	Roald	23	M	Romano	31	M
Rhys	25	M	Roanna	27	F	Romee	29	F
Ria	19	F	Roarke	41	M	Romilda	36	F
Rianna	30	F	Robert	33	M	Romola	29	F
Ric	21	M	Roberta	34	F	Romuald	30	M
Ricarda	36	F	Roberto	39	M	Romula	26	F
Ricardo	41	M	Robin	31	B	Ron	20	M
Ricca	25	F	Robina	32	F	Rona	21	F
Riccardo	44	M	Robindalgar	56	M	Ronald	28	M
Rice	26	M	Robine	36	F	Ronan	26	M
Richa	30	F	Robinson	43	M	Ronda	25	F
Richard	43	M	Robyn	29	B	Ronelle	36	F
Richelle	45	F	Rocco	27	M	Rongo	33	M
Richenda	44	F	Roch	26	M	Ronnie	39	F
Richette	43	F	Roche	31	F	Ropata	26	M

Rorke	40	M	Ruby	21	F	Sadie	20	F
Rory	31	M	Rudiger	46	M	Sadira	25	F
Rosa	17	F	Rudolph	40	M	Sadoc	15	M
Rosabel	27	F	Rudy	23	M	Sador	21	M
Rosaleen	35	F	Rudyard	37	M	Safford	33	M
Rosalia	30	F	Rue	17	F	Saffron	34	F
Rosalie	34	F	Ruel	20	B	Saflyah	33	F
Rosalind	38	F	Rufena	29	F	Sagar	19	M
Rosalyn	32	F	Rufus	22	M	Sage	14	B
Rosamond	36	F	Ruggiero	55	M	Saisho	26	F
Rosamund	33	F	Rugina	34	F	Saki	22	F
Rosane	27	F	Ruihi	38	F	Sal	5	M
Rosanna	28	F	Ruik	32	M	Saladin	24	M
Rosanne	32	F	Rula	16	F	Salaidh	27	F
Roscius	32	M	Ruma	17	F	Salaome	21	F
Roscoe	30	M	Rumon	27	M	Saldia	19	F
Rose	21	F	Rune	22	M	Saleh	18	M
Rosel	24	F	Rupert	35	M	Salema	15	F
Rosemarie	49	F	Ruperta	36	F	Salena	16	F
Rosemary	42	F	Ruprecht	46	M	Salid	18	M
Roseta	24	F	Rupulle	33	M	Salida	19	F
Rosetta	26	F	Rurik	41	M	Salih	22	M
Rosh	24	M	Russel	22	M	Salim	18	M
Rosia	26	F	Russell	25	M	Salisbury	36	M
Rosina	31	F	Rusty	22	M	Sallie	22	F
Rosita	28	F	Rute	19	F	Sally	15	F
Roslyn	31	F	Rutger	35	M	Salma	10	F
Ross	17	M	Ruth	22	F	Salmon	20	M
Rosslyn	32	F	Rutherford	61	M	Salome	20	F
Rouge	30	F	Ruy	19	M	Salomon	26	M
Rowan	26	M	Ruza	21	F	Salus	9	F
Rowandana	37	F	Ruzena	31	F	Salvador	47	M
Rowena	31	F	Ryan	22	M	Salvator	45	M
Rowland	33	M	Ryder	34	M	Salvatore	50	M
Rowley	35	M	Ryland	29	M	Sam	6	B
Roxana	28	F	Rymer	34	M	Samala	11	F
Roxanne	37	F	Sabella	16	F	Samantha	23	F
Roxie	35	F	Sabin	18	M	Samara	17	F
Roy	22	M	Sabina	19	F	Samaria	26	F
Royce	30	M	Sabine	23	B	Samaritana	34	F
Royston	36	M	Sabra	14	F	Sampson	25	M
Roza	24	F	Sabrina	28	F	Samson	18	M
Rozelle	39	F	Sacha	14	B	Samuel	17	M
Rozina	38	F	Sacharissa	35	F	Samuela	18	F
Ruaidhri	52	M	Sachi	22	F	Sanborn	29	M
Ruanuku	35	M	Sachiko	39	F	Sancha	19	F
Ruark	33	M	Saddam	15	M	Sancho	24	M
Ruben	24	M	Sade	11	F	Sancia	20	F

Sander	25	M	Scot	12	M	Serica	28	F
Sanders	26	M	Scott	14	M	Serilda	32	F
Sandler	28	M	Scout	15	M	Serle	23	M
Sandra	21	F	Seabert	25	M	Seth	16	M
Sandy	18	B	Seaforth	38	M	Seton	19	M
Sanford	32	M	Seamus	15	M	Sevilla	44	F
Sanson	19	M	Sean	12	B	Seville	48	F
Santa	10	F	Seanne	22	F	Seward	25	M
Santje	15	F	Searle	24	M	Sewell	22	M
Santo	15	M	Seaton	20	M	Seymour	35	M
Sapphira	43	F	Seaward	26	M	Shadrack	38	M
Sapphire	47	F	Seba	9	M	Shahid	31	M
Sappho	30	F	Sebald	16	M	Shai	19	M
Sapta	12	F	Sebastian	27	M	Shaina	25	F
Sara	12	F	Sebastiane	32	F	Shaine	29	F
Sarah	20	F	Sebert	24	M	Shakur	33	M
Saraid	25	F	Sedgewick	50	M	Shallum	23	M
Sarama	17	F	Sedgwick	45	M	Shalom	23	M
Sargent	30	M	Sedna	16	F	Shamus	18	M
Sargon	29	M	Sefa	13	F	Shana	16	F
Sarid	24	M	Sefton	25	M	Shanahan	30	M
Sarita	23	F	Seirian	39	F	Shanais	26	F
Sarika	23	F	Seiriol	42	F	Shandy	26	M
Sarona	23	F	Selby	18	M	Shane	20	B
Sasha	12	B	Seldon	24	M	Shani	24	F
Saturday	28	F	Selena	20	F	Shanna	21	F
Saturn	21	F	Selina	24	F	Shannon	31	B
Saturnia	31	F	Selma	14	F	Shanti	26	F
Satya	12	F	Selway	22	M	Sharen	29	F
Saul	8	M	Selwyn	26	M	Shari	28	F
Saula	9	F	Semele	23	F	Sharleen	37	F
Sauveur	44	M	Semira	29	F	Sharlyn	34	F
Savage	37	M	Sena	12	F	Sharolyn	40	F
Saville	44	M	Senalda	20	F	Sharon	30	F
Savina	39	F	Senan	17	M	Sharron	39	F
Sawyer	28	M	Senta	14	F	Shasta	14	B
Sax	9	M	Seonaid	31	F	Shaun	18	M
Saxby	17	M	Septima	29	F	Shauna	19	F
Saxon	19	M	Septimus	32	M	Shaw	15	M
Sayer	23	M	Serafina	37	F	Shay	17	M
Scarlet	24	F	Serafino	42	M	Shayna	23	F
Scarlett	26	F	Serah	24	F	Sheba	17	F
Scholem	30	M	Seraphina	46	F	Sheehan	33	M
Schuman	25	M	Serena	26	F	Sheelah	31	F
Schuyler	39	M	Serene	30	F	Sheena	25	F
Scilla	20	F	Sereno	31	M	Sheila	27	F
Scipio	35	M	Serge	27	M	Shelah	26	F
Scobie	26	M	Sergius	35	M	Shelby	26	B

Sheldon	32	M	Sileas	20	F	Somerset	33	M
Shelley	32	B	Siloam	24	M	Sonia	22	F
Shelly	27	B	Silva	36	F	Sonja	14	F
Shem	18	M	Silvana	42	F	Sonya	20	F
Shen	19	M	Silvanus	45	M	Sophia	32	F
Shenae	25	F	Silver	49	F	Sophie	36	F
Shepley	36	M	Silvester	57	M	Sophocles	40	M
Sheree	33	F	Silvia	45	F	Sophronia	52	F
Sheridan	42	B	Simeon	30	M	Sophus	26	M
Sherlock	46	M	Simon	25	M	Sorcha	28	F
Sherman	33	M	Simona	26	F	Sorel	24	M
Sherrill	47	F	Simone	30	F	Sorell	27	M
Sherry	39	F	Simonette	39	F	Sorrel	33	F
Sherwin	42	M	Simpson	33	M	Sosanna	20	F
Sherwood	44	M	Sinbad	22	M	Soter	23	M
Sheryl	33	F	Sinclair	40	M	Spain	23	M
Shih	26	M	Sine	20	F	Spangler	38	M
Shima	23	M	Sinead	25	F	Sparrow	38	M
Shirley	42	F	Siobhan	32	F	Speed	22	M
Sholto	26	M	Sion	21	M	Spencer	35	M
Shona	21	F	Sirena	30	F	Sperata	26	F
Shoshana	31	F	Sirkka	42	F	Sperling	46	M
Shou	18	M	Sirri	37	F	Spero	28	M
Sian	16	F	Sisile	28	F	Spicer	34	M
Sibella	24	F	Sissy	19	F	Spira	27	F
Sibila	25	F	Sita	13	F	Spiro	32	M
Sibly	22	F	Siusan	20	F	Spofforth	51	M
Sidney	31	M	Siva	33	M	Sponner	39	M
Sidony	32	F	Sixte	23	M	Spring	38	F
Sidonie	39	F	Sizie	32	F	Squire	35	M
Siegfrid	50	M	Skip	28	M	Sri	19	M
Siegfried	55	M	Skipp	35	M	St Clair	28	M
Sienna	26	F	Sky	19	F	St John	23	M
Sierna	30	F	Skye	24	F	Stable	14	M
Sierra	34	F	Slade	14	M	Stacey	19	F
Sigfrid	45	M	Sloan	16	M	Stacia	17	F
Sigmund	33	M	Smith	24	M	Stack	18	M
Signa	23	F	Snow	17	M	Stacy	14	B
Signe	27	F	Snowdrop	43	F	Stafford	35	M
Signy	29	F	Snowhite	41	F	Stamford	33	M
Sigourney	52	F	Soane	18	M	Stan	9	M
Sigrid	39	F	Socrates	28	M	Stana	10	F
Sigurd	33	M	Solange	28	F	Standwood	34	M
Sigvard	53	M	Solina	25	F	Stanfield	36	M
Sigwald	30	M	Solita	22	F	Stanford	34	M
Siimon	34	M	Solomon	31	M	Stanislaus	27	M
Silas	15	M	Solon	21	M	Stanley	24	M
Sile	18	F	Solveig	53	F	Stanway	22	M

Star	13	F	Sunny	21	F	Taddeo	22	M
Starbuck	32	M	Suria	23	M	Tadia	17	F
Stark	24	M	Susan	11	F	Taffy	22	M
Starlee	26	F	Susannah	25	F	Taggart	29	M
Starr	22	F	Susanne	21	F	Tahira	30	F
Stavros	42	M	Susie	19	F	Tahiti	31	F
Stean	14	M	Sutherland	41	M	Tahlia	24	F
Steel	16	M	Sutton	19	M	Tahnia	26	F
Steele	21	M	Suvi	35	F	Tai	12	M
Stefan	20	M	Suzan	18	F	Tain	17	M
Stefanie	34	F	Suzanna	24	F	Tait	14	M
Stefano	26	M	Suzanne	28	F	Taka	15	F
Steffi	29	F	Suzette	26	F	Talbot	16	M
Stein	22	M	Suzi	21	F	Talebin	27	F
Stella	15	F	Suzsi	22	F	Talfryn	33	M
Sten	13	M	Suzy	19	F	Talia	16	F
Stephan	29	M	Svein	42	M	Taliesin	35	M
Stephane	34	F	Sveja	30	F	Talissa	18	F
Stephania	39	F	Sven	33	M	Talitha	26	F
Stephanie	43	F	Swain	21	M	Tallara	20	F
Stephanos	36	M	Sweeney	33	M	Tallis	19	M
Stephen	33	M	Sweetie	32	F	Tallulah	24	F
Stephenson	45	M	Swetlana	23	F	Tama	8	B
Sterling	41	M	Swithbert	43	M	Tamar	17	F
Sterne	27	M	Sy	8	M	Tamara	18	F
Steve	35	M	Sybil	22	F	Tamati	19	M
Steven	40	M	Sybille	30	F	Tamba	10	F
Stewart	25	M	Sybilie	39	F	Tammy	18	F
Stiven	44	M	Sybyl	20	F	Tamsin	22	F
Storm	22	F	Syd	12	M	Tana	9	F
Strachan	30	M	Sydney	29	M	Tancred	29	M
Stratford	30	M	Sylgwyn	35	F	Tandia	22	F
Straton	26	M	Sylvain	48	M	Tane	13	M
Stuart	18	M	Sylvania	49	F	Tangerine	48	F
Sturt	17	M	Sylvanus	43	M	Tangila	34	M
Subrahmanyan	47	M	Sylvester	55	M	Tangwyn	32	M
Sue	9	F	Sylvia	43	F	Tangwystl	33	F
Sula	8	F	Sylwen	26	F	Tania	18	F
Sulgwyn	31	M	Syntyche	38	F	Tansy	16	F
Sulien	26	M	Syra	18	F	Tanton	21	M
Sullivan	47	M	Syria	27	F	Tanya	16	F
Sultan	15	M	Tab	5	M	Tapairo	35	F
Sulwyn	24	M	Tabari	24	M	Tapanui	28	M
Sumika	29	F	Tabitha	25	F	Tara	13	F
Sumiko	34	F	Tacita	18	F	Taralga	24	F
Summer	26	F	Tacitah	26	F	Taranga	26	F
Sumner	27	M	Tacy	13	F	Tarati	24	F
Sun	9	M	Tadd	11	M	Tarcoola	31	F

Taree	22	B	Teodorico	50	M	Theodoric	52	M
Tarleton	33	M	Teodosia	34	F	Theodosia	42	F
Tarn	19	M	Tepaea	21	F	Theodosius	45	M
Tarni	26	F	Tepene	29	M	Theola	31	F
Tarra	22	F	Tepko	31	M	Theon	26	M
Tarrant	29	M	Teporo	35	M	Theone	31	F
Tarsus	17	M	Tepotatango	44	F	Theophania	52	F
Tasha	13	F	Terauara	31	M	Theophila	49	F
Tasman	14	M	Terence	34	M	Theora	31	F
Tatam	10	M	Terentia	38	F	Thera	25	F
Tate	10	B	Teresa	23	F	Theresa	31	F
Tatia	15	F	Terese	27	F	Therese	35	F
Tatiana	21	F	Tereza	30	F	Theron	35	M
Tatum	12	B	Terrel	33	M	Thetis	27	F
Tauno	17	M	Terri	34	F	Thibaud	29	M
Tautiti	28	F	Terrill	40	M	Thibaut	27	M
Tavis	35	M	Terris	35	M	Thien	29	M
Taylor	28	M	Terry	32	B	Thiess	26	M
Teagan	21	F	Terza	25	F	Thiewie	43	F
Teague	23	M	Tess	9	F	Thimothee	49	M
Teangi	29	M	Tessa	10	F	Thirsa	30	F
Tearle	25	M	Tetley	24	M	Thistle	30	F
Tearoha	32	M	Teuta	13	F	Thom	20	M
Teata	11	M	Tewahoroa	43	M	Thomas	22	M
Teauotangaroa	49	M	Thaddeus	28	M	Thomasa	23	F
Tecwyn	27	M	Thaine	30	M	Thomasina	37	F
Ted	11	M	Thalassa	18	F	Thor	25	M
Teddy	22	M	Thalia	24	F	Thora	26	F
Tedoroa	33	M	Thane	21	M	Thorald	33	M
Tegan	20	F	Thanh	24	B	Thorbert	43	M
Tegwen	29	F	Thanh Phong	57	M	Thorburn	44	M
Tegyd	25	M	Thank	27	F	Thorley	40	M
Tekea	24	M	Thank Danh	45	M	Thorn	30	M
Tekooti	41	M	Thank Tuyen	49	F	Thorne	35	B
Tekura	31	F	Thank Xuan	42	F	Thornton	43	M
Telford	35	M	Thankful	39	F	Thorpe	37	M
Temira	30	M	Thatcher	38	M	Thos	17	M
Temmatenga	32	M	Thea	16	F	Thurlow	36	M
Tempe	23	F	Theano	27	F	Thyra	27	F
Tempest	26	F	Thebe	22	F	Tiaio	27	M
Templar	31	M	Theda	20	F	Tibb	15	M
Templeton	39	M	Thelma	23	F	Tibelda	26	F
Tenae	18	F	Themis	29	M	Tiberia	37	F
Tenille	32	F	Themistocles	49	M	Tien	21	M
Tennyson	36	M	Theo	21	M	Tiernan	36	M
Teobaldo	29	M	Theobald	31	M	Tierney	42	M
Teodor	32	M	Theodora	41	F	Tiffany	36	F
Teodora	33	F	Theodore	45	M	Tiki	31	M

Name	No.	Sex	Name	No.	Sex	Name	No.	Sex
Ueli	20	M	Ungar	25	M	Vaino	43	M
Uffo	21	M	Unity	26	F	Val	26	M
Uggieri	49	M	Unna	14	F	Vala	27	F
Ugo	16	M	Upton	23	M	Valarian	51	M
Ugon	21	M	Urana	19	F	Valborg	50	M
Uilleam	28	M	Urania	28	F	Valborga	51	F
Uilliam	32	M	Urban	20	M	Valda	31	F
Uillioc	36	M	Urbi	23	F	Valdemar	49	M
Ula	7	F	Ure	17	M	Valdus	34	M
Ulalia	20	F	Uri	21	M	Vale	31	M
Uland	16	M	Uriah	30	M	Valeda	36	F
Ulani	21	F	Urian	27	M	Valek	42	M
Ulbrecht	35	M	Uric	24	M	Valence	44	M
Uldricks	43	M	Uriel	29	M	Valentia	48	F
Ulema	16	F	Urien	31	M	Valentina	53	F
Ulf	12	M	Urith	31	F	Valentine	57	B
Ulfer	26	M	Urmila	29	F	Valenty	45	M
Ulfred	30	M	Ursa	14	F	Valeria	50	F
Ulga	14	M	Ursell	24	M	Valerian	55	M
Ulger	27	M	Ursin	27	M	Valerie	54	F
Ulicia	28	F	Ursino	33	M	Valerio	55	M
Ulick	29	M	Urson	24	M	Valery	47	B
Ulima	20	F	Ursula	20	F	Valeska	44	F
Ulisse	22	M	Ursus	17	M	Valetta	36	F
Ulla	10	F	Urszula	28	F	Valgard	47	M
Ulmer	24	M	Urvan	40	M	Vallia	39	F
Ulpirra	41	F	Urvasi	45	F	Vallis	39	M
Ulric	27	M	Usenko	31	M	Valma	31	F
Ulrica	28	F	Usha	13	F	Valmai	40	F
Ulrich	35	M	Ushnisha	36	M	Valmiki	59	M
Ulrick	38	M	Usman	14	M	Valmond	45	M
Ulrico	33	M	Utah	14	F	Valonia	47	F
Ulrika	36	F	Ute	10	F	Valora	42	F
Ultima	22	F	Utu	8	M	Valori	50	F
Uluka	21	M	Uxor	24	F	Valmana	34	M
Ulva	29	F	Uyeda	20	M	Van	28	M
Ulyana	20	F	Uyeno	26	M	Vance	36	M
Ulysses	21	M	Uzair	30	M	Vanda	33	F
Uma	8	F	Uzi	20	M	Vanessa	36	F
Umberto	31	M	Uziel	28	M	Vanetta	38	F
Umei	21	F	Uzza	20	F	Vang	35	M
Umeko	29	F	Uzziah	37	M	Vania	38	F
Umina	22	F	Vaal	27	m	Vanni	42	F
Ummu	14	F	Vachel	42	M	Vanora	44	F
Una	9	F	Vaclav	52	M	Vanya	36	B
Undina	27	F	Vadim	40	M	Vara	33	F
Undine	31	F	Vail	35	M	Varad	37	M
Undurra	34	F	Vaina	38	M	Varada	38	F

Name	Age	Sex	Name	Age	Sex	Name	Age	Sex
Varden	46	M	Verdun	48	M	Villette	51	F
Vari	41	F	Vere	41	M	Vilma	39	F
Varian	47	M	Verena	47	F	Vina	37	F
Varick	55	M	Verge	48	M	Vince	44	M
Varina	47	F	Verita	48	F	Vincent	51	M
Varnava	61	M	Verity	54	F	Vincentia	61	F
Varuna	41	M	Verla	40	F	Vine	41	F
Varus	36	M	Vern	41	M	Vinita	48	F
Varvara	65	F	Verna	42	F	Vinnie	55	M
Vaschka	47	M	Verne	46	M	Vinny	48	F
Vashti	43	F	Verney	53	B	Vinson	48	M
Vasil	36	M	Vernon	52	M	Viola	41	F
Vasili	45	M	Verona	48	F	Violet	47	F
Vasilos	43	M	Veronica	60	F	Violetta	50	F
Vasily	43	M	Veronika	68	F	Violinda	59	F
Vaslav	50	M	Veronique	72	F	Violinna	60	F
Vassilia	47	F	Verra	46	F	Vira	41	F
Vassily	44	M	Verrell	56	M	Virdis	54	F
Vassy	32	F	Verrill	60	M	Virgil	59	M
Vaughan	47	M	Vesna	34	F	Virgile	64	M
Vaughn	46	M	Vespera	50	F	Virgilia	69	F
Veda	32	F	Vesta	31	F	Virginia	71	F
Vedette	45	F	Veve	54	F	Virginie	75	F
Vega	35	F	Vevette	63	F	Viridis	63	F
Vei	36	F	Vevila	62	F	Virna	46	F
Veikko	64	M	Vevina	64	F	Visant	40	M
Veit	38	M	Vic	34	M	Vita	34	F
Vekoslav	71	M	Vicar	44	M	Vitale	42	M
Velda	35	F	Vicente	51	M	Vitas	35	M
Veleda	40	F	Vicki	54	F	Vito	39	M
Velika	50	F	Vicky	52	F	Vittoria	60	F
Velko	53	M	Victor	51	M	Vittorio	65	M
Vellamo	44	F	Victoria	61	F	Vitus	37	M
Velma	35	F	Victorie	65	F	Viva	54	F
Veloneika	67	F	Vida	36	B	Vivian	68	B
Velvet	59	F	Vidal	39	M	Viviana	69	F
Venance	46	M	Vidonia	56	F	Vivien	72	B
Venedict	55	F	Vidya	43	M	Vivienne	82	F
Venetia	49	F	Vigil	50	M	Vlad	30	M
Venice	49	F	Vigilia	60	F	Vladimir	61	M
Venn	37	M	Vijo	38	M	Vladislav	66	M
Ventura	47	F	Viking	63	M	Vlado	36	M
Venus	36	F	Vikki	62	F	Vlasta	30	F
Vera	37	F	Viktor	59	M	Vogel	43	M
Verban	44	M	Vilem	43	M	Volante	44	F
Verbena	49	F	Vilhelm	54	M	Voleta	39	F
Verbina	53	F	Vilhelmina	69	F	Volker	56	M
Verda	41	F	Ville	42	M	Volney	48	M

Volo	37	M	Warda	20	F	Welya	21	F
Vonda	38	F	Wardell	30	M	Wen	15	M
Vonny	45	F	Wardley	34	M	Wen De	24	M
Voula	35	F	Ware	20	M	Wen Hu	26	M
Vychan	46	M	Wargarang	45	M	Wen Li	27	M
Wade	15	M	Warialda	33	F	Wenceslaus	32	M
Wadsworth	41	M	Waring	36	M	Wenchi	35	F
Wagner	32	M	Waris	25	M	Wenda	20	F
Wahleroa	44	M	Wark	26	M	Wendela	28	F
Wainbaru	35	M	Warka	27	M	Wendelin	41	M
Waine	25	M	Warner	34	M	Wendell	30	M
Wainwright	60	M	Warra	25	M	Wendy	26	F
Waitangi	39	M	Warrack	39	M	Wenlock	38	M
Waite	22	M	Warrah	33	F	Wenona	27	F
Wajid	20	M	Warrane	35	M	Wensley	31	M
Wakefield	49	M	Warranunna	44	F	Wentworth	47	M
Wakely	32	M	Warreen	39	M	Weringerong	72	F
Wakil	29	M	Warren	34	M	Werner	38	M
Wal	9	M	Warrina	39	F	Wesla	15	F
Walcott	22	M	Warringa	46	M	Wesley	26	M
Walda	14	F	Warriwillah	62	F	Weston	24	M
Waldemar	32	M	Warroo	36	M	Weylin	34	M
Walden	23	M	Warrun	32	M	Whetu	23	M
Waldo	19	M	Warwick	43	M	Whiangaroa	52	M
Walford	34	M	Washington	49	M	Whistler	42	M
Walker	34	M	Wat	8	M	Whitaker	50	M
Wallabari	34	M	Waterman	32	M	White	29	M
Wallace	21	M	Watson	20	M	Whitney	41	B
Wallis	22	M	Watt	10	M	Wilberforce	62	M
Wally	19	M	Waverley	57	M	Wilbur	33	M
Walmond	28	M	Wayamba	21	M	Wilda	22	F
Walsh	18	M	Wayland	26	M	Wilder	35	M
Walta	12	F	Wayne	23	M	Wilfred	41	M
Walter	25	M	Weaver	47	M	Wilfreda	42	F
Waltier	34	M	Weber	26	M	Wilfrid	45	M
Walton	22	M	Webster	29	M	Wilga	25	F
Walwyn	26	M	Weema	20	F	Wilhelm	37	M
Wambalano	28	F	Weeronga	43	M	Wilhelmina	52	F
Waminda	29	F	Wei	19	M	Wilkin	42	M
Waminoa	31	F	Weiss	21	M	Wilkins	43	M
Wan	11	M	Welby	22	M	Willa	21	F
Wanda	16	F	Welcome	31	F	Willard	34	M
Wandjuk	30	M	Welda	18	F	Wille	25	M
Wanetta	21	F	Weldon	28	M	Willem	29	M
Wang	18	M	Wellington	50	M	Willi	29	M
Waratah	27	F	Wells	17	M	William	34	M
Warburton	42	M	Welsh	22	M	Willis	30	M
Ward	19	M	Welton	26	M	Willmot	32	F

Name	No.	Sex	Name	No.	Sex	Name	No.	Sex
Yoko	30	F	Zadok	30	M	Zenanda	29	F
Yolanda	27	F	Zahid	30	M	Zenas	20	M
Yolande	31	F	Zahir	35	M	Zenda	23	F
Yolla	20	F	Zahra	27	F	Zenia	28	F
Yooneeara	45	M	Zaid	22	M	Zenith	37	F
Yooralia	42	F	Zaidee	32	F	Zeno	24	M
Yoorana	35	F	Zaira	28	F	Zenobia	36	F
Yootha	30	F	Zak	20	M	Zenobias	37	M
Yoram	27	M	Zakelina	43	F	Zenovia	56	F
Yorick	45	M	Zako	26	M	Zephan	34	M
York	33	M	Zales	18	M	Zephaniah	52	M
Yoshiko	48	F	Zalman	22	M	Zephirah	55	F
Yoshio	37	M	Zamir	31	M	Zera	23	F
Yoshishisa	51	M	Zamira	32	F	Zerelda	35	F
Young	28	M	Zamora	29	F	Zerlina	40	F
Yoyangamalde	51	M	Zana	15	F	Zerlinda	44	F
Yrjo	23	M	Zander	32	M	Zero	28	M
Ysabel	19	F	Zandra	28	F	Zesk	25	M
Yseulete	31	F	Zane	19	M	Zetta	18	F
Ytha	18	F	Zaneta	22	F	Zeus	17	M
Yu	10	M	Zanette	28	F	Zev	35	M
Yuan	16	M	Zannette	33	F	Zeva	36	F
Yudesh	28	M	Zanta	17	F	Zia	18	F
Yugany	30	M	Zara	19	F	Zika	29	F
Yul	13	M	Zared	27	M	Zilia	30	F
Yularai	33	M	Zaria	28	F	Zilla	24	F
Yules	19	M	Zavier	54	M	Zillah	32	F
Yulwirree	55	F	Zdena	23	F	Zilpah	36	M
Yung	22	M	Zea	14	F	Zina	23	F
Yung Chiang	55	M	Zebada	21	F	Zinnia	37	F
Yung Chih	50	M	Zebadiah	38	M	Zippora	47	F
Yung Fu	31	M	Zebedee	34	M	Zita	20	F
Yuri	28	M	Zebulon	32	M	Ziv	39	M
Yury	26	M	Zechariah	52	M	Ziva	40	F
Yusher	33	M	Zedekiah	51	M	Zivian	54	M
Yusuf	20	M	Zeeman	28	M	Zizi	34	F
Yutta	15	F	Zeke	29	M	Zoe	19	F
Yves	35	M	Zela	17	F	Zofeyah	41	F
Yvette	43	F	Zelda	21	F	Zofia	30	F
Yvonne	50	F	Zelia	26	F	Zohar	32	M
Zabad	16	M	Zelig	32	M	Zohara	33	F
Zabrina	35	F	Zella	20	F	Zoltan	25	M
Zac	12	M	Zelma	21	F	Zomelis	36	M
Zachariah	48	M	Zelman	26	M	Zona	20	F
Zacharias	41	M	Zelotes	30	M	Zonar	29	M
Zachary	37	M	Zemira	36	F	Zorah	24	F
Zack	23	M	Zena	19	F	Zoran	29	M
Zada	14	F	Zenaida	33	F	Zoroaster	47	M

Index